CORE
PERFORMANCE
GOLF

CORE
PERFORMANCE
GOLF

THE REVOLUTIONARY TRAINING AND NUTRITION PROGRAM FOR SUCCESS ON AND OFF THE COURSE

MARK VERSTEGEN
AND PETE WILLIAMS

FOREWORD BY TOM LEHMAN

RODALE

© 2008 by JOXY LLC

Rodale books may be purchased for business or promotional use or for special sales. For information, please write to: Special Markets Department, Rodale Inc., 733 Third Avenue, New York, NY 10017.

Printed in the United States of America

Rodale Inc. makes every effort to use acid-free ⧖, recycled paper ♻

Book design by Susan Eugster
Interior photographs: page vi © Robert Galbraith/Reuters/Corbis; other interior photographs © David Zickl
Illustration on page 73 by Sandy Freeman; data for photo illustration on page 23 provided by the Titleist Performance Institute using TPI 3-D

Library of Congress Cataloging-in-Publication Data

Verstegen, Mark
    Core performance golf : the revolutionary training and nutrition program for success on and off the course / Mark Verstegen and Pete Williams.
        p.   cm.
    Includes index.
    ISBN-13 978–1–59486–604–3   hardcover
    ISBN-13 978–1–60529–695–1   paperback
    1. Golf—Training. 2. Physical fitness. 3. Nutrition. I. Williams, Pete, date II. Title.
GV979.T68V47 2007
796.352—dc22   2007039917

Distributed to the trade by Macmillan

2   4   6   8   10   9   7   5   3   hardcover

2   4   6   8   10   9   7   5   3   1   paperback

We inspire and enable people to improve their lives and the world around them
For more of our products visit **rodalestore.com** or call 800-848-4735

CONTENTS

FOREWORD

By Tom Lehman

When I first entered the PGA Tour I never took conditioning that seriously, like most of the other golfers. But, as I entered my second decade on tour, I remember someone telling me that conditioning was the wave of the future in golf. "Okay, once the future arrives then I'll think about it," I remember musing.

But that gentleman was right, and despite my success on tour, I wish I had committed to conditioning earlier. In golf, bodies seem to break down all at once, and in 2001, after a series of knee injuries, I sought the help of Mark Verstegen and his staff at Athletes' Performance in Tempe, Arizona. I expected nothing more than a rehabilitated knee; instead, I left AP armed with a long-term program that I believe will lengthen my career and productivity on the PGA Tour.

Mark's Core Performance program, which you'll learn in this book, will make you a better golfer. It's that simple. You'll work on developing your core strength, spending a lot of time on your hips, shoulders, and midsection, and you'll find yourself feeling more balanced than ever before.

Golfers underestimate the importance of balance at their peril. The weaker you are through the midsection and hips, the harder it is to execute a fierce, balanced swing. As

I reached my early forties, I realized that after following through I was off-balance, costing me swing speed and accuracy. But after following Mark's program, I recovered my balance, allowing me to swing even harder and stay even, which translated into hitting the ball longer and straighter.

Golfers have always hesitated to embrace conditioning; historically, most golfers believed that developing too much muscle mass and thickness would impede their flexibility and diminish their games. And, to a certain extent, that belief is accurate—a bulky frame *does* hurt your swing. But not all conditioning regimens are created equal, and Mark's program will help you build strength *and* increase flexibility—without bulking up.

This program isn't just about getting fit and playing better golf; it's about injury prevention. I've had three or four knee surgeries and the pain and constant pounding almost caused me to give up the game. Since I began following the Core Performance Golf program, not only has the pain dissipated, but I can run and do the cardio work—what Mark calls Energy System Development—that you'll learn in this book.

Golfers sometimes aren't thought of as athletes. We're respected for excelling at a sport that taxes body, mind, and spirit, but we're not thought of like NFL or NBA players.

But golfers are athletes, and this program will make you feel like one.

I remember training with Mark at Athletes' Performance and watching an NFL player do a drill where he jumped up onto a raised box. It was a test to measure explosive strength and power, two things he had in abundance. The rest of the people in the gym, which included some prominent pro athletes, watched in awe.

After I finished my workout, I decided to try the drill myself. I was able to leap onto the box. I probably didn't look as powerful and graceful as the NFL player, but I had discovered the same type of athleticism.

Hey, I'm an athlete. If you don't think of yourself as one right now, you will after following this program.

If you've watched the PGA Tour over the past decade, you know that Tiger Woods has brought training to the forefront. He's the proof that you can get stronger and maintain flexibility. A lot of guys have adopted that approach, but the whole point is to stay committed for the long haul.

The Core Performance Golf program will give you the complete approach that pros like me learn firsthand from Mark, everything from strength and power to flexibility and nutrition. This is no mere weight-training and dieting plan—*Core Performance Golf* will help you lose weight and build lean muscle mass, improving your body composition and functional strength, and, as a result, your golf game.

The beauty of this program is that it's portable; you can take it anywhere. You don't need a lot of equipment, and most of the workouts you'll find within can be completed in a hotel room as easily as they can in your den. What's more, the plan is easy to fit into your schedule, and can be completed in as little as 10 minutes.

Core Performance Golf emphasizes Mark's signature routine—Movement Preparation. It's an active warmup, a series of exercises much more effective than traditional static stretching. These moves might look a little quirky on the practice green, but it's worthwhile to take a moment to find a small private area in the locker room or clubhouse gym to complete the routine—it will all be worth it as you watch the strokes disappear off your handicap. If you commit yourself to Mark's program, you will see the fruits of your labor and come to believe that anything is possible on the golf course.

Golf is all about maximizing flexibility and strength; lacking either will only lead to frustration and injury, to say nothing of wasted greens fees. But *Core Performance Golf* will help prevent injuries and allow you to play this wonderful sport at a level you probably never thought possible.

INTRODUCTION

If I promised to add 25 yards to your drive and make your short game more accurate, what would you say? What if I told you that you could play pain-free, with more energy and vigor as you attack the back nine? What if I swore you could achieve and sustain greater energy and power in all aspects of your life? What would that be worth to you?

The good news is that you don't have to purchase a new set of clubs, hire an expensive swing coach, or painstakingly break down your swing and rebuild it from scratch. Instead, everything you need is in this book.

It goes without saying that golf requires extraordinary skill. It's humbling, exhilarating, frustrating, and joyful. Everyone who's ever picked up a club has wanted to unlock the mystery of a great golf game; but there's no mystery to reveal. The key is simply to discover—and replicate—your most efficient swing mechanics. Consistency is the name of the game.

Most golfers, even some of the top PGA and LPGA stars with whom I've had the honor of working, have never addressed the core fundamental movement patterns that allow them to attain their best swings. They ignore the physical limitations—reduced flexibility, mobility, and stability—that not only decrease their ability to store and release energy—but also produce pain and injury. Golfers are on an endless search for the Holy Grail of swing mechanics—a search that is futile if they haven't taken their bodies through the journey that allows them to express their true swing.

This fruitless quest drives the golf industry, forever telling us that we need the latest club, the most dynamic ball, the newest video, and the priciest instructors. We're grateful for these new breakthroughs; I wish other sports were so tech-savvy. But while new products, equipment, and other innovations *may* help keep golfers competitive, we need a look inward to *definitely* realize our untapped potential, to train our bodies to perform optimally, and to resist injury.

To get the most out of this book, the first thing you need to do is recognize that you're not a golfer; you're a golf *athlete*. It's easy to think otherwise: After all, the history of golf is replete with characters like John Daly, Craig Stadler, and Colin Montgomerie, who have thrived despite large physiques, to put it mildly. Even Phil Mickelson, one of the top golfers of this era, did not always commit himself to fitness; and the great Jack Nicklaus was considered a superlative golfer, but not a great athlete. But despite those successes, all golfers, from the best-paid pros to weekend warriors, must embrace physical fitness to play—and live—at their peak potential.

At Athletes' Performance, we work with the top champions in sport, including golfers of all levels. But no matter what their level of play, golfers who visit AP fall into two categories: those who recognize the need to improve their athleticism so they can drive the ball farther and enhance their performance through improved conditioning; and those players so passionate about golf that they've driven their bodies into the ground by playing and practicing so much. Typically the latter have pain in their lower back, knees, shoulders, and elbows, preventing them from playing the game they love. Common to both groups is an understanding that proper conditioning is integral to withstanding and recovering from the physical rigors of golf, and crucial to realizing your full potential on the course. Integrating the Core Performance Golf system into your life will help you achieve both.

Consider this program the last frontier to boosting your performance. After all, if you're like most golfers I know, you've exhausted every source to improve your driving and short game. You've purchased gadgets, read countless golf magazine articles, and spent hours on the range.

Golfers often accept pain as a badge of honor, but that belief only undermines their games. Tight hips sabotage a golf swing and lead to a chain reaction of biomechanical events that produce back pain. It shouldn't be that way, and it doesn't have to. Moreover, nothing is more frustrating to a golfer than nagging ailments afflicting the back, shoulders, and neck—all of which result from countless hours on the course and at the range. Not only do these ailments slow down your swing speed, they keep you from performing well and enjoying the game. (To wit, some golfers suffer from lower-back pain so severe that they switch to longer putters to limit how far they need to bend over to putt—but what sort of short game do you think they might be able to muster in that condition?)

But hours of practice are not the most common source of golf-related injuries: According to several recent studies, only about one-quarter of golf injuries are due to overuse; 75 percent of injuries result from poor swing mechanics. Unfortunately, most people interpret that to mean they just need some work with a club pro or swing coach. That's only going to exacerbate the problem. Instead, they need to build stability and mobility in their hips, shoulders, and midsection. The good news is that exercises designed to do exactly that are at the heart of the Core Performance Golf system.

Even if you're happy to write off as insignificant whatever discomfort you suffer from playing the game, can you look in the mirror and convince yourself that these ailments haven't affected the quality of your swing and mental preparation? In truth, these nagging aches and pains are like the hazards on a course. That sore elbow is like hitting out of the rough. That back twinge is like hooking the ball into the water. Adjusting your swing in a constant effort to work around the pain is like hitting from a bunker. You can negotiate the hazards, but it's a lot easier to play the ball long and straight, shooting for the pin instead of trying to fight the course at every turn.

It's time to stop doing battle with the wrong weapons. *Core Performance Golf* is not a gimmick; it is a proven system requiring you to approach your mindset, nutrition, movement, and recovery as crucial aspects of your golf game. It challenges you to recognize the importance of what you do from the time you wake up to the time you go to bed and accept proper training and nutrition as the foundation of your best golf—the complete game.

Let's define "best" golf. I imagine that at some point in your golfing life, you've enjoyed your personal round for the ages. Your mind was clear, your stroke was effortless, and your shots dropped perfectly. Perhaps the course was an ideal match for your game, perhaps you were just "in the zone" that day. Whatever the reason, you played better than you thought possible.

The difference between one perfect day and being a world-class golfer, as is the case with any endeavor, is consistency. The pros can perform at an elite level on the toughest courses and against fierce competitors every week. Everyone else gets out there whenever they can, hoping to play respectable golf, and dreaming of that perfect round.

I didn't write this book to help you reach the professional tours, though if you're on that journey, this program will help get you there. The rest of us can learn from the sport's top champions by taking the strategies they use to be the best in the world and applying those tactics to our everyday lives, discovering how to live and play and feel like a top champion in the game of life.

Golf broadcasters are forever talking about how a top pro has a complete approach to the game. But golf, by nature, is a one-sided, ballistic, rotational sport. With courses forever trying to pump more players through to be profitable, you're forced to take a cart. So instead of walking, you take a shot and drive to the next one. Throughout the round, and afterward, you're bombarded by food and drinks that don't contribute to your golf performance, let alone to your overall health.

There's also this perception that after walking off the 18th green we're mentally exhausted from the challenge of the round. This often is perceived as physical exhaustion as well. Yet if we look at the modern game of golf, with increased practice times and the passive cart-riding style that more closely resembles polo than the golf many of

the champions grew up playing, we have a game that leaves one side of the body over-developed, twisted, with poor posture and very low levels of fitness for the amount of time spent enjoying the sport.

Golf is a lifetime endeavor, yet we aren't doing enough to ensure that we can play a long time. We're so worried about the quality of the game that we forget the quality of health and life that the game is built upon. What makes golf so special and adds to its mystique is all of those correlations to life that get plastered on motivational posters. That it's about focusing on the process, taking the good with the bad, playing any lie, letting go past mistakes, etc.

The goal of this book is to help you create a complete game plan for both golf and life, to use golf as the motivating factor to improve the quality of your life and health in general. Most people lack the motivation to get serious about their fitness; but in my experience, golfers, more so than athletes in any other sport, allow the game to permeate every aspect of their lives. So let golf be your motivation, and you will see results, on and off the course.

For instance, when I tell avid golfers, whether promising junior players or business executives, that it's necessary to work out using the Core Performance Golf program three to five times a week for 30 to 60 minutes at a stretch, they tell me they don't have time. After all, they barely have time to *play* golf.

But when I suggest that the time invested will decrease their handicap and improve driving distance by 25 yards or more, well, suddenly they're anxious to start.

I don't just want you to be a better golfer. I want you to be a *healthier* golfer. *Core Performance Golf* is about teaching you the Core Fundamentals to perform both in sport and in the game of life. Your golf and your health go hand in hand, and it's possible to boost both with a limited investment of time and money—but with a serious commitment to your game and your well-being.

This program will help you develop what we'll call a "perfect day." It will organize your day and week, and provide systems to improve your mindset, movement, nutrition, and recovery. This not only will improve the quality of your life but also give you greater potential to shoot brilliantly every time you go out, bringing you closer to a consistent, world-class level.

I don't expect you to devote your entire life to improving your game, but I want to empower you with simple solutions that will help you make significant progress, whatever the state of your game and your physical condition. *Core Performance Golf* will improve your swing and your mental approach, introducing you to the latest in sport science, and laying the foundation for great success on the course. This is no mere swing tinkering; *Core Performance Golf* will teach you how to properly move your body to take advantage of your current swing. Concerned with more than your swing, your short game, or your waistline, *Core Performance Golf* will help prevent pain, maximize your gifts, and point the way to great success in golf and the game of life.

Let's tee this thing off!

GOLF/GAME OF LIFE

IN

PERFORM

TO

CORE FUNDAMENTALS
MINDSET. NUTRITION. MOVEMENT. RECOVERY.

PART 1

CORE PERFORMANCE
GOLF MINDSET

CHAPTER 1

FORE!

I love working with golf athletes because they're so focused on the processes and the minute details that go into their games. When I start talking about movement patterns, about tweaking a body position 5 to 10 degrees, it resonates with them in a way unlike it would with athletes from other sports, who tend to focus on where their bodies are positioned in space or on the field. Successful golf demands that you get in the correct position to achieve the proper swing plane. The exercises in this book, which help you achieve that goal, make sense to athletes who already take a movement-based approach to their sport.

I also have great respect for the golfers' mindset, which demands that they feel accountability and take responsibility for their own performances. They recognize that they alone are ultimately responsible for identifying and addressing factors limiting their games. The golf culture prizes persistence and dedication to achieving long-term goals.

At the same time, the insistence on precision and fanatical attention to detail common among golfers are in themselves limitations to be overcome. Successful golfers can suffer "paralysis through analysis" caused by countless hours of instruction, harsh self-assessment, and obsessive attempts to refine swing mechanics, not realizing that mechanics may not be the problem. The result is frustration, even desperation.

Such single-mindedness prevents golfers from looking off the course and exploring how their physical fitness affects their game. Many golfers pay more attention to preventive maintenance of their cars than they do to tuning their bodies to perform the best in the game they love.

Golf is a lifetime sport, yet too many treat their bodies—their most important golf equipment—without respect. In no other aspect of their game would this be acceptable. Would you take pride in playing with a cracked shaft or a dented clubface? Of course not!

PREVENTIVE MAINTENANCE IS KEY

Golf athletes rarely consider the damage that the sport's repetitive movement inflicts on their bodies, to say nothing of taking proactive measures to prevent injury and improve performance. Since golf emphasizes movements on only one side of the body, playing the game inevitably creates muscle imbalances that lead to a laundry list of injuries, ailments, and long-term deterioration and pain.

Golfers often assume that their problem is back pain, when often the hips are the root cause. If your hips are tight and inflexible, you're going to have a tough time playing effectively. If you have back pain, chances are you have far less flexibility in your lead hip, which endures the most traumatic force at the end of each swing. Over time these forces, resulting from poor, inefficient movement patterns, cause wear and tear on your muscles and joints, much like excess miles on a car.

Poor mechanics produce injuries. But when I talk about mechanics, I'm not referring to the adjustments suggested by your golf pro or swing coach. Instead, I'm talking about the three-quarters of all golf injuries that come from playing a lot of golf with poor, inefficient movement patterns.

As I mentioned before, many golfers come to Athletes' Performance because they have played for years without engaging in significant preventive maintenance, and their bodies have broken down as a consequence. They arrive shocked and surprised that their lower backs have given out, forcing them to the sidelines. Frustrated and impatient, they want to quickly fix whatever is afflicting them so they can head back out on the course, where they would inevitably settle into the same routine that led them to us in the first place. Naturally this is no kind of solution—the definition of insanity is doing the same thing and expecting a different result, a maxim as true on the golf course as off.

Several years ago, a top PGA Tour player arrived at our facility on the recommendation of a fellow pro. Though only in his midthirties at the time, he was considering retiring from the tour because his body no longer allowed him to pursue his lifelong passion. He was terribly shaken by the likely prospect of having to give up everything he had worked so hard for from the time he was a child. Saddest of all was that no one had taught him the Core Fundamental movement patterns that he needed to perform at his best in golf and in life. Not having the benefit of these techniques resulted in long-term deterioration, robbing him of not only his physical ability but also the determination that had made him a champion.

So often it takes a defining moment like this to stimulate long-term change. Thankfully, he quickly recognized the benefit of the Core Performance Golf system and implemented its techniques in his training regimen. He not only got back on his feet but soon embarked on some of his best years on the PGA Tour.

This episode made me realize that if some of the biggest names in golf do not understand how to prevent pain and maximize performance despite strong financial resources and access to the finest professionals, then it is all the more likely that recreational players do not either.

INTEGRATING THE CORE FUNDAMENTALS

The goal of *Core Performance Golf* is to give you proactive systems and strategies that will serve as the foundation for realizing your potential and playing your best golf safely for a lifetime.

Core Performance Golf also emphasizes your health off the course. Perhaps you grade the quality of your health by your ability to play at your best. But as valuable as golf is in many respects, it contributes little to cardiovascular health. Could it be that golf has given you a false sense of your vitality and physical condition?

I've heard people conflate golf and exercise, and, to a certain extent, golf can be valuable and invigorating physical activity. But playing a round of golf is not a particularly effective means of improving your cardiovascular system—and it's essentially useless if you use a cart rather than walking the course. Effective exercise requires that you be honest with yourself—and that you

(continued on page 8)

THE CORE PERFORMANCE GOLF BREAKTHROUGH

BY NATALIE GULBIS

When I first arrived at Mark Verstegen's Athletes' Performance several years ago, I was coming off an illness that had caused me to lose 12 pounds and left me feeling weak and lethargic.

With the LPGA season approaching, I needed to get my weight and strength back as soon as possible. The Core Performance Golf system not only helped me recover my strength, energy, and weight, it provided me with an integrated lifestyle system that's fueled my performance on the tour and in life.

This program is not just about how to best spend an hour in the gym, though even that would be tremendously beneficial. It's also about how to approach rest, sleep, recovery, nutrition, stress, travel, and everything else that affects your physical and mental well-being, especially as it pertains to golf.

Many golfers experience back pain and I was no exception. The discomfort in my back was sometimes excruciating. I was afraid to do any back exercises out of fear that I might hurt it even more. But by following this program, I was able to strengthen my core—my hips, midsection, and shoulders—and the back pain went away. Not only that, I corrected a lot of the muscle imbalances, asymmetries, and deficiencies hampering my game. I now hit the ball farther and have the flexibility to lengthen my career and protect me from injury.

Before instituting this regimen, I was training inefficiently, spending a lot of time and getting little return. With the Core Performance program, I learned not only how to create a lean, powerful physique, but also a body optimized for golf and resistant to the ailments and injuries so common to our game.

The thing I love about Mark's exercises is that they're so functional. You can feel immediately how they're relevant to golf and how they're strengthening and stabilizing your body, giving you more mobility and flexibility. The exercises also target more areas of the body, which enables you to accomplish more during your workout in less time.

That's important whether you're a businessperson, a stay-at-home parent, or a touring professional. I'm on the road constantly and the Core Performance program is completely portable. Even on those rare occasions where I can't get to a gym, I know I can perform the body-weight version of the workout, especially Movement Prep, an active series of warmup exercises that I do at the beginning of my Core Performance workouts, before a round, or on those days when I'm incredibly busy but still want to exercise. I've performed the Movement Prep routine alongside hotel swimming pools, on the beach, even in a hotel hallway. It takes just 5 minutes and makes such a difference.

Sometimes Movement Prep is part of my Regeneration days, a key concept of the Core Performance program. I used to train every day, thinking that more was better. I was tired and sore all the time and figured that was the price I needed to pay to be the best. Now I've learned that if I take the time to get proper sleep and spend those Regeneration days in a state of "active rest," getting massages, using a foam roll, and doing things that support my recovery, I'm going to be in much better position to thrive in golf and every other aspect of my life.

Since that first trip to Athletes' Performance, I've come to understand the importance of nutrition. One of Mark's analogies I always remember is to look at your body as a high-performance car, like a Ferrari. You wouldn't put cheap gas in the car, let it run on fumes, and drive it into the ground. Yet this is what many of us do to our bodies.

The idea is to create lean body mass, or muscle, that effectively propels you and gives you constant energy. You could have two women who both weigh 130 pounds with dramatically different body compositions. Despite their identical weights, the one with more muscle and lean mass is going to have more energy and be better equipped to deal with challenges and play better golf.

The Core Performance program will show you how to assemble your meals with the proper mix of protein, carbs, and healthy fats. You'll learn how to fuel your body for an effective workout and, just as important, what to consume afterward for optimal recovery. You'll even learn what to eat before, during, and after a round of golf.

No matter what your schedule, you can tailor this plan to work for you and you'll see an immediate improvement in your game. Golf is a game of consistency and the best compliment I can give the Core Performance program is that it's made me a much more consistent player, capable of performing at my highest level each time I go out. Regardless of your goals in golf and life, the Core Performance system will provide you with the structure and the means to reach those goals in the most efficient way possible.

know that swinging a light implement 100 or so times in one direction will not significantly improve your health.

So, ask yourself: Have you done anything to improve the quality of your movement patterns? Or have you caused more dysfunction and asymmetries in your body because of the way you warmed up and the way you swung your club?

Has the culture of golf and the faulty perception that golf is itself an effective workout clouded your judgment about your overall fitness level? Have you made the right choices when it comes to the nutritional options you typically consume before, during, and after your rounds?

Just as you take the time to address the strengths and weaknesses of your game, step back and consider your approach off the course. This will provide a more complete picture of what needs to be done to improve the quality of your health *and* the quality of your game. The two go hand in hand.

Have you spent thousands of dollars upgrading clubs, in effect updating your software, when you've invested little in your body, the hardware that acts as the foundation for your golf success?

Do you believe you have the most effective system to address the factors limiting what you're truly capable of? Can you look in the mirror and confidently say that you've left no stone unturned in your quest to improve your performance and that you've investigated the most cutting-edge solutions and strategies to better your mindset, nutrition, movement patterns, and your ability to recover?

If you can truthfully answer all these questions in the affirmative, then good for you. But if you can't, don't worry—this book will introduce you to techniques that will improve your game and your overall health. That's the true reward: After all, the ability to shoot the round of your life is one thing, but improving the quality of your life and health on a daily basis—that's something else entirely, and something far better.

STABILITY AND YOUR SWING

The body does a phenomenal job compensating for weak areas. This might seem like a good thing, but these compensatory movement patterns and "energy leaks" are not our friends. Your body is just trying to work around a lack of stability or mobility, or to pick up the slack of muscles that have been turned off, thus putting more stress on other muscles. This is not a good thing.

These energy leaks affect your swing. Even if only a few small but critical muscles are shut off and locked down, your swing will suffer.

How does this happen to an active golfer? It's simple: There's lots of standing in golf, as in life, and people often sit into their hip, transferring weight to one side of the body and sitting on their tissues. You do it without even thinking, whether to get comfortable, to strike a pose, or just to pass the time. But this seemingly innocuous habit has negative consequences: Over time, these muscles shut off, creating an area of instability around your hip.

This has a huge impact on your swing mechanics. As you go into your backswing, your backside hip has decreased stability, limiting your ability to store energy in the hip cuff. The back hip slides laterally and creates an unstable foundation, which increases volatility in your swing and puts undue stress in your hip joint, down your iliotibial (IT) band, into your knee and foot, and into your lower and mid back. You're still going to be able to swing, but every time you do so, you're putting more wear and tear on all the supporting muscles and bones.

Even more damaging is continuing to walk or run with these movement patterns, as the hip rides bone-on-bone, causing inflammation and greater stress in all the muscles above and below the hip. This leads to pain and, over time, may require surgery or physical therapy.

But fear not—if you are aware of the problem and know that there's a simple solution that takes just a few minutes, a few times a week, you can head this off, improve your swing, and decrease the effect of these inefficiencies. Starting with the next chapter, we'll identify the solutions.

CHAPTER 1 SUMMARY: Golf athletes typically wear themselves into the ground by continuing to play with improper movement patterns, leading to hip and back problems. Through the Core Performance Golf system, you can prevent this by applying the Core Fundamentals—the mindset, nutrition, movement, and recovery that create and sustain excellence. The program will enable you to work out more efficiently, thus improving performance on the golf course and increasing resistance to injuries and long-term deterioration.

CHAPTER 2

SELF-EVALUATION

Golf is a humbling sport, even for the best players. Others never attempt it or give up on it because it's too much of a struggle. They assume they can't master the game because they're uncoordinated or lack the time and talent to play at even a rudimentary level.

My coauthor, Pete Williams, is one of those people. Pete has been around golf all his life. He has taken lessons from talented club pros, has a good understanding of swing mechanics, studied the sports psychology of golf, and lives in Florida, one of the sport's hotbeds. He played sports in high school and remains an active, well-conditioned recreational athlete.

And yet, until recently, Pete could not play golf. He was brutally bad. His game was pain-

ful to watch. Interestingly, Pete's problem had nothing to do with swing mechanics or the mental aspect of the game, but rather that his hips were so locked down and inflexible he was virtually incapable of executing a proper address, let alone a golf shot. He could have hired the best swing coach and a top sports psychologist and it wouldn't have mattered.

When Pete arrived at Athletes' Performance to help write our first book, *Core Performance,* I had him lie on a table as I tested his hip and hamstring flexibility. He was one of the tightest people I'd ever seen. Several of our interns working nearby stopped what they were doing to marvel at this utter lack of flexibility. One wanted to use Pete as a case study for his graduate thesis.

Rather than subjecting him to that indignity, I placed Pete on the Core Performance program. He never will be a contortionist, but over the years he's managed to improve his flexibility, loosen and mobilize his hips, eliminate the back pain that had plagued him, and even play passable golf. Pete's improvement had little to do with additional golf instruction and a lot to do with creating the core stability, mobility, and movement patterns needed to play golf.

Many golfers suffer the same frustrations as Pete, and perhaps you're one of them. But no matter where you are with your golf game, you're probably not reaching your fullest potential.

That's why I want you to spend a few moments doing some simple self-evaluations. These tests will expose weaknesses in your body that affect your game. Even if you're a scratch golfer, you may fail some of these tests. If so, that's reason to get excited, because you have a lot of room for improvement.

How is that possible? Even if you play at an elite level, you may not be able to play 36 holes and make it look effortless. You may tire after 18 holes, which makes you no different than most everyone else. The difference between you and the people who can go 36 without breaking a sweat is that they expend far less energy than the average golfer—and it has nothing to do with their fitness level or how hard they swing. The difference is that their bodies are so much more mobile, stable, and efficient. In short, they're able to efficiently create explosive energy. These self-assessment exercises are the first step to closing the gap and maximizing your game.

FUNCTIONAL MOVEMENT SCREEN TESTS

The Functional Movement Screen tests were developed by Gray Cook, a physical therapist and strength coach in Virginia who has been a pioneer in the field of movement and performance. A good friend and colleague, Gray and his FMS team are official partners of Athletes' Performance, and I urge you to check out his book, *Athletic Body in Balance: Optimal Movement Skills and Conditioning for Performance,* if you're looking for further information in this area.

Deep Squat

The first test is the deep squat (see page 14). Think of a top PGA touring pro squatting on the green, reading his next putt. While the ability to deep squat successfully might help you read putts better, it has more important applications to golf. If you can deep squat successfully, you probably have good overall flexibility. If you can't perform a deep squat, you're probably stiff throughout the body or you have asymmetry—an imbalance between the right and left sides, and front and back sides—a common by-product of playing golf. On the surface, these asymmetries might not seem like a problem, but successful golf requires that you be able to load up on both sides of your body with ease. By improving your ability to squat, you'll improve movement when shifting weight from left to right, a key part of golf.

When your body is balanced, your golf swing is effortless, but asymmetries require your brain to constantly rewrite the software governing your swing and compensate so you can execute a decent shot. Sometimes it succeeds, sometimes it doesn't, but either way it robs you of mental and physical energy. To conserve and best expend energy, balance is required.

The deep squat test does not emphasize one's ability to transfer energy from one side of the body to the other, but it does require maximum range of motion in the hips, shoulders, and torso.

Straight Leg Raise

This test (see page 15) combines leg flexibility with torso strength and stability to identify asymmetries. When your core functions properly, the trunk and pelvis stabilizers fire before the hip flexors. This helps stabilize the spine, which is important since the spine plays such a vital role in the golf swing. If you lack core stability and strength at this point, don't worry. You'll improve it considerably through this program.

Seated Rotation

This test (see page 16) shows how tightness in one area can affect the movement of another area. If you find it difficult to get into a cross-legged position, you'll flex and contort your spine to take stress off your hips. That reduces your spine's ability to rotate left and right. If your hips don't seem tight, but the seated rotation is still difficult, your spine likely lacks flexibility. That manifests itself in difficulty rotating right and left.

Don't worry; the Core Performance Golf program will fix this problem.

(continued on page 17)

DEEP SQUAT

1 In a doorway, place a strip of tape on the floor 1 foot from the doorjamb. Stand centered in the doorway, facing the doorjamb with your feet shoulder-width apart and parallel to each other, with half of your body on each side of the door and your toes touching the tape. Hold a golf club overhead so that your elbows and shoulders are at a 90-degree angle with the club. Press the club up and extend your elbows to a straight position. If you hit the top of the door with the club, finish extending your elbows as you descend into the squat position.

2 Descend slowly into a full squat position as deep as you can go. Your heels should be flat and your feet should not turn outward or slide as you descend to the full depth of your squat. The club should remain overhead at all times—make sure that neither the club nor your face or head touch the doorjamb. To successfully complete the squat, your heels must remain on the floor, your head and chest must face forward, and you must press the club as far overhead as possible. Give yourself three attempts to successfully perform the movement.

3 If you can keep your heels down, prevent your feet from sliding or rotating, bend your hips below your knees, and keep your knees aligned over your feet, without allowing the club to touch the wall, congratulations—you've passed your first test. (But stop immediately if you feel any pain at any point.)

STRAIGHT LEG RAISE

① Lie on your back through a doorway, with your arms at your sides, palms up, and your head flat on the floor. The midpoint between your hip and the top of your knee should be in line with the door frame.

② Lift the leg closest to the door frame while keeping your foot flexed and knee extended. The other leg should remain on the floor and not move. Place a golf ball under your fixed knee to keep your leg in place; you don't want to compensate through your hips and back. Your head and hips should remain flat on the floor, and your arms should not move. Do the test three times on each side.

③ You've succeeded if the anklebone of the lifted leg clears the door and your other leg does not move. Your opposite foot should point upward throughout the entire test and the knee should remain extended.

SEATED ROTATION

1 Sit cross-legged on the floor, your back straight, and leaning slightly forward. One foot should be on each side of a doorjamb. Hold a golf club above your chest in front of your shoulders. It should touch your collarbone and the front of both shoulders at all times.

2 With your back straight, rotate to each side. Attempt to touch the club to the door frame. Maintain an upright position and limit leaning toward the door or bending your spine in any direction.

3 Your aim is to touch the club to the wall while keeping it level and in contact with your chest. Your spine should remain stable and upright.

DECONSTRUCTING THE SWING

I want you to return to the prior three tests throughout this program. As you progress through the Core Performance Golf system, you'll find them easier. More important, your ability to successfully complete these tests will translate into better performance on the golf course.

If you are capable of these movements, your swing will follow. Golf writers and fans love to talk about how top touring pros rebuild their swings time and time again. Perhaps you do the same thing with your game. The difference is that, unlike the top touring pros, you may not have established the Core Fundamentals to construct the swing that's going to elevate your game. You might have a perfectly good swing, but if you can't execute the motions that will allow you to replicate that swing, then it's of no use to you.

Instead of obsessing over rebuilding your swing, you should examine the physical nature of what goes into the modern-day golf swing and what you can do. If you can master the Core Fundamentals, you'll be in much better position to take advantage of your golf pro's expertise during lessons. Otherwise you're not making the most of the pro's wisdom, and, quite frankly, you're wasting your money.

The physical examination of the swing begins with the address. Your position at the address may be the most important variable in establishing consistency, ensuring that

I posture   C posture

your body creates and repeats the swing you're trying to achieve. Golfers typically assume an address position with their feet directly underneath their hips, which are slightly rolled under, and their backs and shoulders rounded. Their torsos end up looking more like C's than I's, which is *not* what you want.

Instead, place your feet slightly *outside* your hips for greater stability. Your feet should feel like they're physically gripping the ground, like an eagle's talons gripping a tree branch. This grip will initiate and activate all movement that happens up the kinetic chain. ("Kinetic chain" is a fancy way of saying that everything in the body is connected and related, allowing us to transfer energy from one part of the body to the next, starting at the feet and working up.)

Shifting your focus up the kinetic chain, you should keep your legs slightly unlocked, with your knees over your toes so that you can ideally position your hips and pelvis. Rather than rolling your hips forward, in keeping with conventional wisdom, keep your hips and pelvis tilted up and back. That should help shift your weight so that you are evenly balanced over the arch of your foot. This leaves you in a more "athletic" stance.

Your body should be leaning slightly forward so that your chest is balanced over your feet, and your back should be straight. The term we use at Athletes' Performance is to "feel tall through your spine." That doesn't mean keeping your torso perpendicular to the ground; instead, tilt forward so you feel like you're in traction from your pelvis through the top of your head. This will better position your spine to rotate around the center axis and maximize the number of muscles able to consistently store and release energy. This position will allow your torso to work in concert with your hips to generate greater clubhead speed, in a more efficient, fluid manner.

Traditionally, golfers rounded their shoulders forward, with the shoulder blades and arms reaching down toward the club and ball. Because of this position, shoulder and neck injuries have plagued golfers—that's why rotator cuff injuries are so commonplace, among duffers and pros alike.

The problem with this position is that it robs you of any ability to store energy. To correct this flaw, instead of rounding your shoulders, I want you to "feel tall" by elevating your sternum (breastbone) slightly so that your shoulders fall more naturally back and down. Imagine that you're trying to drop your shoulder blades into your back pockets by relaxing your trapezius muscles.

Keeping your shoulders in this position decreases the potential for injuries and allows you to generate greater arm speed in your swing to store more energy to be released on your downswing. Your head should be "aligned with your spine"; this is critical to your ability to consistently rotate above the center axis. It also improves the consistency and quality of information you assimilate visually and otherwise as you complete your swing. Your head position is vital to establishing your balance along the center axis of rotation.

Hip position is *the* biggest component of the address as it allows you to develop power from your lower body, specifically your hip cuff, and create consistently powerful swings. Your thighbone and pelvis are surrounded by more than 40 muscles in and around your hip, 40 percent of which cause either internal or external rotation. These muscles govern your hip's ability to rotate around your legs and put muscles on stretch so they will store, and ultimately release, energy.

In the traditional posture, with your hips rolled forward, you lose almost all ability to store and release energy in both hips as you rotate around the center axis. This causes most golfers to rotate through their ever-vulnerable lower back, using only the muscles along the spine and arms in an attempt to create the rotation and with it clubhead speed. This posture limits your spine's ability to turn and twist at every point. It minimizes your ranges of motion and significantly increases the amount of stress throughout your spine and shoulders, leading to back and shoulder strain that together account for most golf injuries. To avoid these pitfalls, place your hips in the proper address position so they can store and release energy from the lower kinetic chain.

Under the old swing model, weight is transferred back to the right side of a right-handed golfer. The lead leg would rotate and turn the knee in toward the back leg, often coming up on the front toe, and then slide and shift back on the downswing for impact. The modern swing, however, emphasizes even weight distribution across your feet with proper pelvic

PELVIS/HIP CUFF

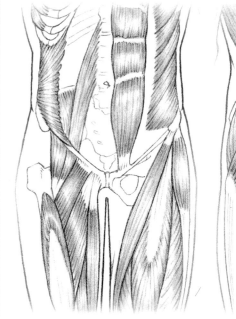
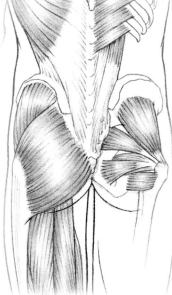

● More than 40 muscles attach to the hips and pelvis (not including the pelvic floor)

● 16 of these muscles externally or internally rotate the hip (approximately 43 percent of all lumbo-pelvic/hip muscles)

position. Your legs should be slightly flexed and remain in this position throughout your swing. As you take the club away, keep your lead leg *away* from the back leg.

Why is this so important? Much like the resistance in a coiled spring, it helps store energy in the internal rotators of your front-side hip cuff. When you rotate to your back-swing, you store energy in the external rotators of your back-leg hip cuff. The resulting stretch around your pelvis is how you store energy, like a rubber band, in the 40 muscles in and about your hips that are primarily responsible for creating rotational, segmented acceleration. The back-side hip cuff is the trigger to your swing. As you take the club away and rotate your pelvis, you will feel a stretch in the posterior hip cuff and your hips will slightly initiate or "trigger" the downswing motion, creating a greater "X factor" with your shoulders, storing more energy in your torso, which is unleashed through your arms and transferred into the club.

The best way to understand the "X factor" is to imagine standing on an observation deck looking directly down on Tiger Woods at the tee. As his club comes back, his shoulders turn more than his more stable hips, which will fire and rotate toward the ball first, but only for a brief instant. At that instant, from your vantage point, his body would form the letter X. He's able to disas-

Coil your spring during the backswing

sociate his shoulders and hips as he moves across the transverse plane to generate incredible power. Tiger has developed extraordinary mobility and stability, and he efficiently channels energy through pillar strength—more on that in a moment.

Just as you position your feet to be in line with the target in the address position, we want you to line up your body for an optimal swing, creating the potential to store and release energy efficiently and consistently through your kinetic chain. A stable and centered position will be the foundation to a centered, well-balanced, consistent swing.

X factor

By establishing this platform, you'll have the potential to consistently replicate an athletic swing. If this foundation isn't there, you have little chance of hitting the ball well from one shot to the next.

THE KINETIC CHAIN AND THE DYNAMICS OF THE SWING

Under the traditional swing model, the lead leg would pivot, turning in toward the back leg, causing golfers to reach and turn as high as possible, straining to create a big rotation in the shoulder—the "X factor." The swing included a pause at its apex, trying to get an extra degree or two of rotation, and then required transferring energy from the hands down by sliding the hips forward.

The problem with this method is the intricate timing required to execute it properly. As a golf athlete, you know that the majority of what dictates hitting a shot straight and long is the path of the clubface through the impact zone. But in utilizing the old swing, with your hips sliding back and forward, your impact zone moves with your hips. If you consider how precise the interaction of your hips, shoulders, arms, and clubface need to be upon impact to hit the ball squarely, it's like the planets have to align for you to hit it straight.

This method is not impossible; in fact, it's a testament to the persistence and hard work of many golfers that they've been able to perform using the traditional swing. But wouldn't you rather adopt a more fluid, natural model? Instituting the Core Performance Golf physical foundation for the swing will help keep your feet, knees, hips, and shoulders on the same center axis, optimizing a slight lateral shift back and forth. That way, you have the potential to generate club speed efficiently, stay consistently centered on the ball, and boost the amount of time the clubface stays square throughout the impact zone. This makes your swing less volatile, allowing you to consistently hit the ball straight.

So what should you feel in the backswing? As the club sweeps back, your lead leg should stay *away* from your back knee. It's almost as if you're pushing the lead knee *down* so that you store energy in the internal rotators of that lead-leg hip cuff, feeling a stretch across the groin. In the old model, when your lead leg caves in, you lose the ability to store energy in your hip and leg. By keeping your lead leg over your toes, you'll feel a stretch in the inside part of your groin, which is like a whole ball of rubber bands storing energy for your downswing.

By shifting your back leg, rotating your pelvis around it, you should feel a stretch deep within your hip, storing your potential energy, like pulling the hammer back on a gun. This hip cuff will be the initial "trigger" to the downswing.

Moving up the kinetic chain, your shoulders should turn to finish, loading up the potential elastic energy in your torso. As you do this, your left shoulder blade slides away from the spine, storing even more energy to help generate greater club speed. The old swing required you to pause at the top of your swing, releasing or dissipating all of this stored elastic energy.

With your new athletic swing, you won't pause at the top of your swing. Here the hips initiate the downswing movement, which is hard to recognize with the naked eye. But the back hip cuff is the trigger to the downswing; your hips slightly leading your shoulders increases the "X factor," or the amount of stretch between your hips and shoulder, which then causes your shoulders to more rapidly follow. Your arms and club soon follow.

The golf swing, as fluid as it looks, is a lot like braking with your car. Your hips, as you come closer to impact, come through and slow down. It's as if you've slammed on the brakes. When you do that, the car may stop, but the driver continues to fly forward.

In golf, this process is a good thing. When the hips stop, the energy transfers to the shoulders and they too decelerate briefly prior to impact to allow all of this stored energy to transfer into the arms, which also decelerate rapidly. This causes the clubhead to whip through, bringing all these forces together at the instant of impact, transferring your body's energy through the ball. This aspect of the modern swing is why golf athletes are driving the ball record distances, taking advantage of advances in golf technology.

Just as a driver's education instructor will tell you, you want to avoid violent stops by easing off on the brakes and slowing gradually. That's what happens after impact with the ball in the golf swing. You ease off the brakes, dissipating all this energy, across all these segments, and bringing the body to a smooth and safe stop as you finish the swing.

As technical and intimidating as this may

TPI 3-D SWING ANALYSIS

A golf swing is a dynamic series of movements that must be linked efficiently together. Learning how to store and release energy through your body's kinetic chain will help you take your swing to the next level.

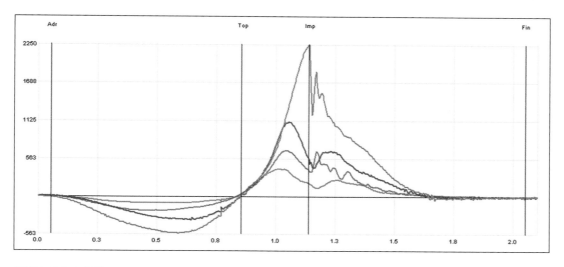

7.6 PlvAngVelLocAx 6.3 TrnkAngVelLocA 0.0 ArmsRtSpVS   0.0 ClbRtSpVS

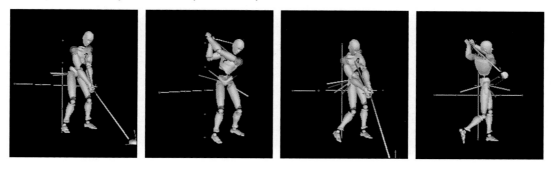

sound, this motion is efficient, fluid, dynamic, and easily repeatable. Remember, you want to avoid pausing at the top of your swing—that counterproductive act releases the muscles' stored energy that you so desperately need for the downswing.

Instead, understand that when you take the club back, you're moving in a manner that already initiates the downswing, which stores more energy in the kinetic chain, releasing it into the ball. Top pros who follow the Core Performance Golf system feel like their backswing is diminished. Yet when they review the swing on video and overlay it with their old swings, they'll notice that the club is within a few degrees of that top position. They've been able to create a more elastic swing, better storing potential elastic energy and releasing it efficiently into the ball.

These techniques will help improve your game, but if you try to integrate them without first undergoing the Core Performance Golf program, you'll have little shot at success. First you need to train your body so that you possess the stability and mobility to produce this movement. The Core Performance Golf program will improve your body's ability to get into a quality address position. It will help you maintain balance, improve your stability and mobility, and increase your ability to store and release energy elastically.

Many golfers think they should only worry about their dominant side, and if golf is your primary source of physical activity then your right or left side will be overdeveloped, and the other underdeveloped. Over the long haul, this decreases your potential to produce an efficient swing since your body is dominant on one side. There's no elasticity remaining in the "rubber bands" that form the muscles on the other side of your body. By creating balance between your right and left sides, you'll ensure that as you take the club away your muscles go on stretch, giving you the potential to store and release this energy.

The Core Performance Golf program is designed to build your body so that you can efficiently produce an effective, repeatable swing while decreasing the potential for common golf-related injuries. This is not a traditional fitness program repackaged. It's been scientifically engineered and tested by the top scientists and champions in sport, and it can be applied in a simple, fun, yet challenging way, whether in a corner of your home, the clubhouse, or the gym.

Core Performance Golf is a completely integrated game plan that should permeate your life and act as the foundation to improving your swing and protecting your body so that you can continue to improve and enjoy your game for a lifetime.

CHAPTER 2 SUMMARY: Even some of the most accomplished, gifted athletes lack mobility, stability, and some of the Core Fundamental movement patterns to thrive in golf and avoid long-term ailments and deterioration. Through some basic self-evaluations, it's possible to recognize these specific limitations and create a system that will allow the body to operate with maximum efficiency. By creating a balanced body, targeting asymmetries, we'll be able to transfer energy efficiently from our left to our right sides and optimize our golf swings.

PART 2

CORE PERFORMANCE
GOLF MOVEMENT

A STRONGER SHAFT

Golf manufacturers put a lot of resources into developing clubs with strong, elastic shafts. Naturally, you want to make the most of this technology. The good news is that the most important shaft can be developed at far less cost and is the most sophisticated weapon in your bag.

That "shaft" is your body's "pillar strength," one of the central tenets of the Core Performance system. Pillar Strength is the foundation of all movement. It consists of the complete integration of your hip, torso (or core), and shoulder stability. Think of a mannequin with no limbs. Those three areas give us a center axis from which to move. If you think of the body as a wheel, the pillar is the hub and the limbs are the spokes.

We want the hub to be perfectly aligned and stable so we can draw and effectively transfer energy throughout the body, whether playing golf or just dealing with life's demands. It's impossible to move the limbs efficiently and forcefully if they're not attached to and controlled by something solid and stable.

There's a reason why parents are forever telling kids to sit up straight. Without what I call "perfect posture," you will significantly increase the potential for injury in a "pain chain" that starts with your lower back, descends to the knees and ankles, and rises through your shoulders, neck, and elbows. Not surprisingly, those areas are among the most common locations for golf ailments.

The Core Performance system trains body *movements* instead of body parts, as many bodybuilding-based workouts do, is because everything about the body's engineering is connected. What happens to the big toe affects the knees, hips, and ultimately the shoulders. Many workout programs do more harm than good by producing muscle imbalances and inefficient movement patterns that sabotage the body's highly coordinated operating system.

The Teaching Pro Says . . .

KEEP YOUR POSTURE PERFECT

In order to maximize the benefit of the exercises in this book and maintain your body's stability and mobility over the long term, it's important to maintain perfect posture. There are several measures you can take throughout the day to support this goal.

The first thing to do is keep your tummy tight, not just while exercising but all day. Keep your stomach flat against the hip bones, as if pulling your belly button off the belt buckle. This isn't the same as sucking in your gut and holding your breath. Keep the abdominals in, but still breathe.

Second, keep your shoulders "back and down." Think of dropping your shoulder blades into your back pocket. Another way to think of it is elevating your chest so your shoulders naturally drop back and down. As people age, they tend to flex forward, as if their chests are caving in. Instead you want to do the opposite, almost as if there's a fishhook inserted under your sternum and pulling up. This allows your shoulders to fall into place and provide perfect posture. The exercises in this program require you to bring your shoulders back and down, but you'll want to make that a daily habit.

You also want to "keep your hips tall." You want to "feel long and tall" from your hips to your head. Think of pulling a flexible straw to make it as tall as possible.

The goal of instituting perfect posture is to create Pillar Strength—the integration of the shoulders, torso, and hips, which creates the potential for efficient and powerful movement in golf and in life.

Bodybuilding-based workouts view the physique as a series of parts, and most people tend to think of movement as starting from the limbs. When we reach out to grab something, we think of those motions as originating with the end result—we've reached out, therefore, we've used our arms.

But movement starts from the center of the body, the core area of the torso. That's why we refer to the torso as the pillar—its alignment and function directly correspond to the quality and efficiency of every movement, especially in golf.

You already know how important it is to stabilize your feet outside your hips and grip the ground with your feet; how vital it is to align yourself in the address position to store and release energy through your swing. You also know how important it is that you stay in perfect balance throughout your entire swing, as you twist around your center axis to produce a consistent swing plane. Now you'll learn that Pillar Strength is the foundation of these fundamental motions and positions.

Pillar Strength is the one thing that you cannot live without. If a golfer—or any kind of athlete—were to focus on just one thing to help optimize performance, Pillar Strength would be it. Pillar Strength is the complete integration of your hips, shoulders, and torso working together to produce efficient movement patterns. If you ever look at an anatomy book you will notice that these three areas are woven together through an intricate figure eight that crosses your body from the left hip to the right shoulder and vice versa with muscular and fascial (connective) sheets that create the foundation for human movement.

We talked about the importance of the address and the pain and poor performance that come from a pillar shaped like a "C." The anatomical inability to rotate from this C pillar—and severe limitation of the ability to optimize stored potential energy—is not only going to make it hard to play effective golf but may also lead to a number of other long-term and short-term health problems.

Core Performance Golf focuses on your hips, torso, and shoulders with isolated movements designed to innervate or "turn on" these critical muscles, and later integrate them into more functional golf movement patterns. Some of these movements focus on certain muscles in and about your pillar and later integrate them back into coordinated multi-joint, multi-plane activities—first and foremost, your swing.

The pillar is the common denominator among everyone who walks through the doors of Athletes' Performance. Even in world-class athletes, the pillar is the one area that has taken the most abuse and received the least amount of care. By focusing on the pillar and these postural elements, we have the greatest return on investment (ROI)—both ROI per exercise time and the ROI that correlates directly to your performance on the course.

The following simple test is the best illustration of the importance of stability, mobility, and efficient elastic movement patterns: Place your left hand on a flat surface, preferably a table. Raise your middle finger, as if initiating the backswing. Now push it down as hard as you can, as if you were driving through the ball. Really slam that finger down.

Try this drill five times and see how much speed you can generate. This is the equivalent of the old-fashioned golf swing. It didn't feel or sound too powerful, did it?

Now tweak the exercise: Leaving your left hand on the table, reach over with your right hand, pull that same finger back and let it snap down. You can feel the stretch, storage, and release of energy and hear the obvious difference. The second method required less effort and generated so much more force.

If you were to continue raising your middle finger under its own power, you'd get tired. But lifting it with your other hand enables you to do it all day long and produce far more power with a fraction of the effort.

This is a good illustration of elastic power, the very sort of store-and-release process required to play effective golf. The more efficiently you can store and release energy, the less effort you have to expend.

Stability is the foundation of elasticity and is derived from the improved coordination produced when you focus on the small stabilizing muscles in and around your joints, specifically your hips, torso, and shoulders. If you were to lift your finger up but not stabilize your hand against the table, your whole hand would elevate and you would not be able to store energy in your finger.

The same holds true for your swing. If you don't have a stable base, starting at your feet, working up into your hips and torso, you lose the ability to put muscles on stretch. You'll notice this with golfers who have loose swings. They seem like they have a lot of motion in their swings, but it's not always channeled and there's little club speed at impact. As you watch these swings, you think it's a miracle they make consistent contact with the ball.

Stability allows you to have a fixed point from which to stretch the muscle, so it can efficiently store and release energy. Otherwise, you're like that loosey-goosey golfer, swinging randomly and hoping for contact.

The other part of the elasticity equation is mobility, which is a limiting factor for many who play the game. To illustrate, put your left hand back on the table. If the muscles in your hand are too tight, you might not be able to lift your finger off the table. That restricts your ability to put a muscle on stretch, limiting your potential to store and release energy through your swing.

Golfers with limited mobility must compensate in order to generate motion, which results in some crazy swings. Think of Rodney Dangerfield in *Caddyshack* or any older guy at the course who struggles to take the club back from the address position. (Whatever they lack in physical mobility they tend to make up for with their mouths!)

Once you have created the optimal amount of mobility and stability, you can begin to develop your body to efficiently store and release energy, which not only will help improve your game but also protect your body and train it to better withstand the rapid stretch loads associated with playing golf.

To examine how pillar strength is integrated into the swing, we begin by breaking down the address, initiating movement with the turn and storage of energy in the hip cuff and lower body. By turning the shoulders away, you'll feel a tremendous amount of stretch from the front hip and back shoulder running across the body. Imagine the stretch of the shirt fabric being like a rubber band that stores energy, which is released to initiate the downswing.

To store the energy on the backswing, you naturally release energy sequentially to develop club speed and consistent impact zones. Even though club speed tends to be the greatest focus for golf athletes, the majority of injury and stress to the body occurs post-impact, during deceleration. That's when your body, which is rapidly set in motion through impact, has to slam on the brakes and dissipate energy through the follow-through as you finish with your shoulders and hips pointed down the fairway.

This deceleration leads to a tremendous amount of trauma in the lead hip, torso, lower and mid back, all the way into the shoulders and rotator cuff. It calls on the pillar strength developed through the Core Performance Golf program, which optimizes the performance of your "brakes," the eccentric muscle contractions that decelerate the body. We refer to this "elastic" process as your body's ability to withstand rapid stretch loads.

Everything in this system addresses the vital core areas of the hips, torso, and shoulders. These core areas, perhaps more than anything else, will determine your long-term success and enjoyment of the game.

HIP STABILITY

The hip joints are as critical to a golf athlete's success as the rotator cuff is to a baseball pitcher's. In fact, that analogy is why the hip joint and surrounding musculature are referred to as the "hip cuff." That anatomy provides the hip with stability, mobility, and strength.

The hip cuff is the control unit for your lower body. It governs the thigh, which interacts with your knee and affects your foot position. The centrality of the hip cuff is why tremendous attention must be paid to strengthening the muscles in and around the area, as they are critical in controlling everything below your hips, and everything above as well.

Hips are the most overlooked area when it comes to decreasing the potential for injury and improving performance in golf. Many of the surrounding muscles determine internal and external rotation, which is critical to efficient swing mechanics. But if you're like most golf athletes I've seen, you've probably paid little attention to the muscles of this crucial area, let alone in a manner specific to golf.

Most back and hip problems occur because of improper mobility and stability and faulty utilization of your hips. Most people are locked down or unstable in their hips. If one of your hip capsules is locked down, which limits mobility, it's as if one of your thighbones is welded to your pelvis— imagine wearing a permanent cast on your hip. To get anything to move, you would have to use excessive motion in your knees and back to make up for your hip's immobility. The lower and middle back share some com-

mon responsibilities with your hips, but they were meant to be secondary, not primary, initiators of movement. By maximizing efficiency in and around the hip cuff through improved mobility, stability, and strength, you will discover the engine that will propel every stride and stroke you make on the golf course.

Your hips and gluteal muscles are the most important part of this powerful engine. Your "glutes" are not just there for show; they're built to go. Learning how to use your glutes and all the surrounding musculature in your hip cuff will decrease the potential for injury and improve golf performance.

Your goal is to initiate all movement from the hips while maintaining perfect posture. If you're going up steps, squatting to pick something up, or simply walking, squeeze your glutes until your legs are extended. Walk with your toes pointed forward, your chest over your knees, and your legs extended, creating a straight line from ear to ankle. This way, the pressure is on your hips—where nature intended—not your knees.

The benefit of initiating movement with your hips doesn't stop there. You know the easiest way to get buns of steel? Use them constantly. Look for every opportunity to lengthen and strengthen your glutes, whether it's squatting, hiking up hills or climbing stairs, getting out of a chair, walking, or running. Think of life as one big glute workout, and you'll see amazing results.

The importance of proper hip and pelvic position in the address position is seen in their influence on your knees and the stability of your lower body as you grip the ground. A stable platform at your feet, maintained by keeping your knees over your toes and rotating with the proper pelvic position, will optimally store energy in both your front- and back-side hip cuffs. That will optimize your hip rotational speed, giving more potential for club speed and efficiency.

Don't be surprised to find that some of these small muscles around the hips and glutes have been switched off. You might find that the left or right glute is not firing, and you're not alone. Every world-class competitor who comes into Athletes' Performance has some of these muscles shut off and/or locked down. Rest assured—we will identify and work this area in almost every aspect of this program.

CORE STABILITY

You've no doubt heard the term "core stability." Unfortunately, the phrase has been misappropriated to refer to washboard abs. But abs are just a small component of the middle third of your pillar known as the core. The core consists of the muscles of your torso, primarily your abdominals and lower back. It's the vital link between hip and shoulder stability, and it includes such muscle groups as the rectus abdominis, transverse abdominis, internal and external obliques, erector spinae, latissimus dorsi (lats), and many small stabilizing muscles between the vertebrae of the spine known as the multifidi.

The multifidi are the tiny muscles that often get shut off because of a back injury and never become reactivated, causing long-term back problems. These muscles cannot function alone; you have to help them by training your core muscles to become strong and stable, with the right types of recruitment patterns that will enable them to work in tandem with your shoulders and hips.

Instead of just focusing on the abs, the goal is to create the framework for all movement. The aim isn't just a well-sculpted midsection; it's a high-performance core.

This area plays a pivotal—pun intended—role in your swing. Ideally, all of the small vertebrae that make up your spine should rotate a few degrees and together produce significant rotation. That creates the "X factor," the separation between the hips and shoulders.

But when your torso is not straight and strong, the ability of your hips and vertebrae to rotate is minimized, creating tiny bony blocks, which decreases your ability to put muscles on stretch, thus decreasing the potential for mobility or power. This C-shaped pillar also compromises both the lower back and shoulders. When your torso is in a C position, it decreases your ability to work your hips like the turret on a tank. You end up forcing the spine to compensate in order to generate more motion through the lower back, which ultimately leads to back pain and injury.

Since the torso acts as a foundation for the shoulders, standing in the C position undermines the shoulders, both in golf and in life. Instead of a C pillar, you want to produce an "I pillar." Core Performance Golf will free up the muscular restrictions that cause this C posture by releasing the tight muscles in the front of the body as well as those responsible for rotation.

The movements in the Core Performance Golf program will create long-term change in a body that's been degraded by years of repetitive stress caused by bad posture on the golf course and in daily living. In short, this program will reduce the amount of pain and tension you experience in your torso while playing and in everyday life. Core Performance Golf will allow you to feel tall from your pelvis through your torso and shoulders, which is so important to successful golf. You'll improve your stability and mobility, which will provide the maximum opportunity to store and release energy in your swing.

The short game—specifically, hours spent putting—causes all kinds of aches and pains, usually around the neck and back. I recognize the need to improve consistency around the greens, but if you can bolster your ability to withstand stress, you'll be able to focus on chipping and sinking putts, rather than on the aching muscles hampering your short game and distracting your focus.

In order to maximize the benefit of the exercises in the Core Performance Golf program, it's important to keep your tummy tight, not just while exercising but all day. Think of your tummy flat against your hipbones. Keep your tummy tight by "feeling tall" and slightly pulling your belly button off your belt buckle. This isn't the same as sucking in your gut and holding your breath.

Your abdominal and lower back muscles work as a team. The ringleader is the transverse abdominis, or "TA," which is the first muscle that's recruited each time you move. If you can keep your TA activated and your tummy tight, you'll be well on your way to efficient movement and the prevention of long-term deterioration.

SHOULDER STABILITY

The shoulders take a beating in golf. Take a look at your posture in the mirror. Your shoulders might be rolled in, with your thumbs rotated toward the center of your body. Golf, along with the stresses of everyday life, contributes to this hunched-over position, whether you're sitting in front of computers,

hunkering down endlessly in your car, or waiting out a flight.

If you rush to play golf without activating the muscles that reset the shoulder joint into proper alignment, you'll play with your shoulders rolled in. Before you know it, shoulder pain will crop up during the round, and that's going to affect your play.

We tend to think of the hands and arms as carrying the workload for the upper body, but it's really the shoulders that should bear that weight. That's why we often speak of someone *shouldering* a burden.

There is a lot going on in and around the shoulder joint. The dynamic, ballistic nature of golf is a challenge for a healthy shoulder

complex and dangerous for a dysfunctional shoulder. If your body is in an inefficient, flexed C pillar position, your shoulders will be rounded up and forward, sliding away from your spine and waist and reaching forward and down toward the club. This is a dangerous, inefficient position in which to place the muscles of the rotator cuff. From this poor position golfers repeat a dynamic swing time and again—it's a recipe for shoulder pain.

The Core Performance Golf program addresses the relationship between the torso, shoulders, and hips and helps these three areas work in concert to prevent injury and optimize your swing. We'll focus on specific exercises to isolate and turn on the small muscles in your shoulders to help improve their function and strength and integrate them into your swing.

To begin, remember the importance of perfect posture. Our natural instinct is to drop the shoulders forward, especially after long periods of sitting. But you ought to do the opposite: Elevate your sternum and let your shoulder blades hang back and down, which will give you proper posture.

The exercises in this program will require you to bring your shoulders back and down, but you'll want to make it a daily habit. To make lasting change, you must lengthen your "internal rotators" (chest and lats) and strengthen the "external rotators," the muscles of the upper back, rotator cuff, and the rest of the shoulders.

This posture is the exact opposite of the shoulder shrug, the motion you make when you say, "I don't know." If you make a habit of bringing your shoulders down—think of dropping your shoulder blades into your

The Teaching Pro Says . . .
TAKE AN ATHLETIC SWING

In the traditional swing, you would take the club away, reach and almost hold at the top, then swing downward. Now, using the new method, you're going to feel like you're reaching to the top, but you're going to go back and initiate the downswing, creating a greater X factor, storing and releasing more energy and generating more speed. What many top teaching pros and players note is that the new model cuts down on swing plane deviations because you're not exaggerating the range of motion. What's more, the new model is more natural for the body; the swing attains natural height and repeatable stretch as opposed to a big reach and sometimes futile attempt to fall back into the proper swing plane.

You might feel like that club is only going half as far back as it did using your old swing, but if you compared the two on video, you'd see the body is still going through a similar range of motion during the backswing and initiation of downswing. It will feel like two different swings, but the end club position may not look different. The rest of the body will look different, but the end club position will be the same relative to the torso—the only distinction is that you arrived there by storing and releasing elastic energy rather than with an inefficient big stretch and reach, followed by an attempt pull the club back down. You're using your core strength and stability to swing naturally as opposed to forcing it.

back pockets—you'll be amazed at the results.

Golf coaches stress the importance of the shoulders and arms in an effective swing. When you watch great golfers at the top of the backswing—from the back-side hip, across the back to the lead shoulder—there is a tremendous amount of stretch. Like a rubber band, they store energy that's released on the downswing.

To emulate that sort of swing, you must rely on your lead shoulder. As you go through your backswing, your lead shoulder blade slides away from your spine, taking all the muscles of the upper back and putting them on stretch to later release this energy to generate greater club speed.

The same holds true after impact on the follow-through, where your back-side shoulder slides away from the spine as it hits the brakes to decelerate your arms on your follow-through. This is why the shoulders are so critical to the golf swing and you must integrate the shoulders, torso, and hips to store and release energy and produce a natural, efficient, and consistent golf swing.

Building pillar strength is more than just a few exercises for your shoulders, torso, and hips. It is the foundation for all movement and you must integrate it into your life, not just when you're performing the Core Performance Golf workout. Keep in mind this book's core movements and concepts when you're walking up stairs, hustling to meetings, and lifting children.

No matter how busy you are, you can devote much of your day to improving your pillar, thus improving your on-course performance. Alternatively, if you ignore your pillar, your foundation for movement will gradually erode, gripping you in a downward spiral of pain and inefficiency both on and off the course.

Pillar strength is the foundation of your swing, but diminished pillar strength affects far more than your golf game. In fact, your golf score will seem trivial compared to the pain in your hips, back, knees, and feet, which might ultimately require joint replacement surgery. It's no different than if you had a wobbly front left wheel; the tire ultimately is going to blow. Swinging a golf club 120 times doesn't do the damage as much as the daily wear and tear that's so much a part of life.

CHAPTER 3 SUMMARY: Pillar strength, the foundation of movement, consists of shoulder, torso (core), and hip stability and strength. Strengthening and stabilizing these areas allows our bodies to perform optimally on the golf course and become resistant to injury and long-term damage off the course.

CHAPTER 4

THE 19TH HOLE: REGENERATION

To golfers, the 19th hole refers to the well-deserved psychological relaxation and regeneration at the end of the round. But as with everything else in this book, we want to shift the paradigm and make the 19th hole something that truly helps restore and maintain your energy levels and fully experience the gains you've made from a focused round of golf.

Look at regeneration as the equivalent of recharging your batteries or refueling your tank. If you recognize and follow this simple formula, you will dramatically increase performance.

WORK + REST = SUCCESS

The things you do at rest are just as important as the work you perform. If you focus on having high-quality rest and regeneration, you'll get more return on investment from every minute of your round of golf or workout.

This is likely a familiar concept: After all, we could work longer and, in theory, accomplish more if we did not sleep. But we work far more efficiently and effectively if we sleep 6 to 8 hours. We also could work more hours over the course of a year if we didn't take vacations. Yet most of us discover that we're far more productive if we schedule some time to relax and recharge.

When I talk about rest, I don't mean putting your feet up in the clubhouse and having a cold one. Instead, true regeneration asks you to recognize that you've gone about your game with a world-class system. You now have an open mindset on how to best optimize your system and rituals to play your best golf for a lifetime.

Beyond proper sleep routines, the other half of this equation is optimizing the body's ability to recover from the stresses and demands of practicing and playing golf, as well as the stresses of the game of life.

In order to accomplish this goal, we have to create a system to help the body recover and "regenerate." We don't think twice about cleaning our clubs or recharging the batteries in our cell phones and laptops. I know that the mere act of playing a round of golf, for many people, is a regenerative escape from the grind of everyday life. Many people focus their vacations, if not their retirements, on the game of golf. But golf is not a complete game and does not itself provide sufficient exercise, and at the same time it is too active to provide total regeneration.

Thus far, we've discussed a system to produce our best performance on and off the course. Now we need to expand upon it with some short, focused sessions that will give your body what it needs to recover and regenerate—tactics that you will be able to implement and use for a lifetime.

The regeneration strategy permeates the entire Core Performance Golf system. In the United States, we've developed such a nose-to-the-grindstone mentality when it comes to work that we've become inefficient. We work so hard, with so little time to recover, that our productivity suffers, and ultimately, we break down. We want to be more efficient and enjoy all aspects of our lives more. Regeneration helps that happen.

It's easy to see the regeneration concept at work in some European countries, where businesses close for daily siestas and people typically receive 4 to 6 weeks of vacation a year. You might not agree with the practical aspects of that system, but it's undeniable that such recovery periods lead to a healthier, more energized workforce.

Our approach to recovery and regeneration starts with a commitment to build recovery into each day, week, month, and year. Look for opportunities to allot time for relaxation, whether at work or at home, even if it's only 15 minutes. Focus on such regenerative techniques as self-massage, flexibility exercises, and hydrotherapy (such as hot and cold contrasts). This approach should also hold true in your weekly plan, where you're planning a morning or an evening off or some activity that allows you to psychologically and physically recover, like going for a walk, enjoying a hot tub or bath, or scheduling a massage. More broadly, apply the same concept to each month and ultimately, by building in proactive vacations or breaks, to each quarter of the year or to the holiday seasons.

Golf requires specific recovery and regeneration patterns. The sport has unique demands and produces wear and tear at certain points, likely exacerbated by chronic tightness caused by too much time sitting.

The specific strategies we'll discuss in this chapter address the demanding, dynamic nature of golf and life and provide specific routines that help reset your muscle length to protect your long-term posture. These routines focus on areas that endure significant golf-related stress: the forearm-elbow-wrist area, the shoulder and neck region, hips, knees, and feet, and, of course, the back.

These routines decrease the potential for pain in these areas and give you a proactive game plan to help you perform better, not just by reducing pain but also by accelerating recovery and building strength in these critical areas.

The regeneration unit requires you to purchase some inexpensive items that our top pros include in their travel survival bags. These devices include an STS Bar, foam roll, stretch rope, and tennis ball. Each will help you iron out the muscles involved in your swing, and help maintain great posture. These simple devices can be tossed in your golf or gym bag or occupy a small area of your home. Some of our athletes have found it convenient to place the items in a small basket at the side of a couch, easily accessible when relaxing or watching TV.

Our goal with regeneration is not to do *more*, but to integrate these routines into the relaxation periods you have scheduled in your normal daily routines. I believe that once you try them and experience them, you will look forward to these reinvigorating activities at the end of your round or workday. You'll find instructions for the self-massage and flexibility exercises in Chapter 9.

SELF-MASSAGE

Golf requires you to produce dynamic, ballistic movements and walk through hilly terrain for up to 5 hours, which often leads to tissue trauma and muscle spasms. These spasms result from overstimulated muscles that have been worked too hard.

The foam roll will help you alleviate these spasms. It is an 18-inch-long roll of tightly packed foam, roughly 5 inches in diameter. By rotating and rolling your hamstrings,

(continued on page 46)

GETTING ENOUGH SLEEP

BY SCOTT PELTIN

What if I told you that there was a magic pill that could slow the aging process, increase your energy level, improve your overall health, reduce your risk of premature death, enhance your immune system, make you more mentally alert, and improve your physical and mental performance? Would you believe me? What if I told you that you take it every night, but you may not take enough of it?

This magic pill does exist. It's called sleep.

Getting proper nutrition is crucial, but if you eat a bad meal or even skip a meal, you rarely feel like you're ready to collapse. Regular exercise is paramount, but if you skip a workout, it doesn't weaken your immune system, decrease your mental clarity, or destroy your mood. Sleep, on the other hand, is the foundation of everything we do. It rebuilds our bodies, replenishes our chemical stores, and allows us to stay alert throughout the day.

What impact could sleep possibly have on your golf game? For starters, if your mental clarity is reduced, you're going to be less able to focus on things like wind, varying turf, the pitch of the green, or the many other course conditions you must take into account to play your best. Plus, when you're tired your body must release more adrenaline to keep you awake. This prevents you from being able to relax, remain calm, and stay in control. As your round of golf goes on, you'll likely become physically fatigued, which will directly impact your balance, stability, and coordination.

In 2001, the National Sleep Foundation performed its famous "Sleep in America" survey, determining that 63 percent of adults get less than the recommended 8 hours of sleep per night and 31 percent get less than 7 hours. More than 40 percent of adult Americans reported having trouble staying awake during the day.

PHYSICAL ACTIVITY

PROPER NUTRITION

ADEQUATE SLEEP

Sleep deprivation can interfere with memory, energy levels, mental abilities, and mood. In a study conducted by the University of Chicago Medical Center in 1999, researchers found that the condition drastically affects the body's ability to metabolize glucose, leading to symptoms that mimic early-stage diabetes.

Sleep deprivation also can contribute to heart disease, diabetes, obesity, and cancer. Without sleep you simply cannot function at your best. Sleep debt undermines your ability to eat health-consciously and exercise as well. When the brain is exhausted, it doesn't know whether it is sleep-deprived or starving for glucose, so the natural response is to crave sugar, which is why you have late-night cravings when you're tired. When you're low on energy, your brain wants to conserve energy, so motivation to exercise is greatly reduced.

Sleep occurs in stages, each with a different EEG (brain wave) pattern. While sleep researchers may classify sleep into many stages, there are just two basic forms of sleep: slow wave sleep (SWS) and rapid eye movement (REM) sleep.

As we age, less of our sleep is REM sleep. REM sleep is where dreams occur but the muscles are inactive. SWS sleep is subdivided into four different stages, and is important for many of the restorative functions of sleep.

During the first deep sleep of the night, the greatest amount of growth hormone is secreted to help the body repair the damage that has occurred throughout the day. This may be why being shocked awake within the first hour of falling asleep seems to leave you so worn out the following day.

Newer sleep research indicates that sleep cycles vary throughout the night, with the first and final stages being closer to an hour and the middle stages being up to 2 hours. Even more significant is the finding that it is total sleep that is the final determinant of sleep debt, since the body actually adjusts the length and number of sleep cycles based upon the body's needs that night. This is why consistent sleep patterns are the most conducive to restorative sleep and inconsistent sleep patterns are the most likely to lead to sleep deprivation.

So when you're looking for ways to improve your golf game, don't just look at your swing. One of the most important factors in improving your concentration, consistency, confidence, and focus is getting the right amount and quality of sleep. Nutrition, recovery, and getting proper sleep are vital for keeping you out of the rough and playing your best golf.

Scott Peltin is a founding partner of Tignum AG, a performance institute for corporate leaders and a strategic partner of Athletes' Performance.

quadriceps, back, lats, and hips over the foam roll, you will release these spasms and accelerate your body's recovery.

The foam roll routine is like a massage. It uses deep compression to help roll out the muscle spasms that develop on the golf course. The compression overstimulates the nerves, signaling the muscle spasm to shut off. This allows the muscles to relax and loosen up, gets the blood and lymphatic system flowing, and helps restore healthy muscles.

Tissue is like a rubber band that you want to keep supple and elastic. Unfortunately, it tends to get knotted up with spasms over time. If you put 20 knots into a rubber band, it cannot store nearly as much energy. More stress goes into a few parts of the rubber band instead of dispersing throughout the band. Your goal is to undo the knots and spasms. Once those are worked out, you must address them daily and weekly to make sure that no more knots accumulate. It takes consistent, proactive maintenance.

You'll probably enjoy the foam roll routine—everyone likes massages. Still, there will be some uncomfortable moments, as there are with a professional massage. Once you're past the first few weeks, though, it will become considerably easier and more comfortable. The foam roll is a great barometer of the quality of your muscle and connective tissue. The better it feels, and the less it hurts, the better the quality of your tissue.

As you roll on the foam, discovering muscle spasms and pressure points, you'll knead out the knots by working back and forth for 30 to 60 seconds and then holding on that pressure point for an additional 30 seconds until the muscle cries for mercy and releases from spasm. This will help iron out the muscles used in your swing.

Another item to help you perform self-massage is our versatile Soft Tissue and Stability (STS) Bar. Available at www.coreperformance.com/golf, this simple yet revolutionary device compresses and stretches muscle. It provides an effective self-massage that may be done before, during, or after a round or workout. The STS Bar releases muscle spasms while increasing blood and lymphatic flow in the body. The device has small eyelets on each end that enable you to use the stick for the stability lifting, chopping, and rotation exercises in this program. Thus, you will be able to "lengthen then strengthen" your body to bolster golf-specific movements.

The STS Bar is portable and versatile, so you can take it with you wherever you go and target specific areas of your body. You might use the STS Bar before a round to aggressively work the insides of your forearms for 30 seconds each, and then use it for 30 seconds on the outside of each forearm. This improves your grip by warming up the tissue and activating your proprioceptive system, the sensors in the joints, muscles, and tendons that provide the body with information to maintain balance. If you don't have an STS Bar, grab a rolling pin from the kitchen.

Lastly, you should use a tennis ball for a series of trigger-point, self-massage exercises that will work areas such as your IT (iliotibial) band, thoracic spine, and the bottoms of your feet.

FLEXIBILITY EXERCISES

Self-massage helps untangle knots, but you also must build flexibility, an integral component of the *Core Performance Golf* program. From Movement Prep to nearly every exercise, flexibility is addressed. Active-isolated stretching (AIS), developed by Aaron Mattes to target specific muscles that get short or stiff from the demands of golf and life, will help you dramatically improve your flexibility.

The key to AIS is its *active* nature. To perform the stretches, you won't stretch for 10 to 30 seconds, as in traditional stretching, because that doesn't require your body to actively reprogram itself for new ranges of motion.

Instead, by holding the stretch for just 1 to 2 seconds, the exercises will increase the muscles' range of motion a few more degrees each repetition. Exhale during the hold position, releasing tension and getting a deeper stretch. Return to the starting position and repeat for the prescribed number of reps. With this type of exercise, you have to put your "mind in the muscle" to focus on firing the proper muscles and relaxing the muscles to be stretched.

More than working your muscles, you're reprogramming your brain. As an example, the hamstring stretch requires you to lie on your back, with your hands behind a knee, pulling the knee to your chest. As you extend your knee, those muscles contract, and your hamstrings automatically relax, through a process called reciprocal inhibition. Hold that position for a 2-second count as you exhale and release the tension from your body and mind. Two seconds might not seem like much, especially if you're used to static stretching routines, but this is a gradual process that will yield a few degrees more with each repetition over the course of 8 to 10 reps, ultimately resulting in significant increases.

You also can do AIS exercises using an 8- to 10-foot length of rope, about the thickness of a jump rope. You can go to a home improvement store and have a length cut off for just a few dollars, or you can check out the ropes at www.coreperformance.com/golf.

If you wrap the rope around one foot at a time and perform a series of moves, you will reprogram your muscles to contract and relax through new ranges of motion. For a hamstring stretch, you lie on your back with a rope wrapped around one leg. First pull your toe up toward your shin, then squeeze, or "fire," your quadriceps, hip flexors, and abs. Lift your leg as far as you can into the air. Give gentle assistance by pulling on the rope and then holding for 2 seconds. Return to the starting position and continue for 8 to 10 repetitions.

You should also use traditional static stretching, both post-round and on days when you're not playing. Here we'll hold for 30 seconds to 3 minutes to improve long-term structural flexibility, which affects both the fascial and muscular systems.

However, avoid static stretching prior to a round or working out—static stretching works by putting the muscle and the nervous system in a submissive hold until it shuts off and releases. The last thing you want to do is to have your muscles shut off prior to using them. As a general rule, static stretching should be limited to post-round, post-workout, and days off.

CONTRASTS

At Athletes' Performance, athletes alternate between sitting for 3 to 5 minutes in a hot tub and 1 to 3 minutes in a 55-degree "cold plunge" tub. The cold therapy, in particular, decreases the natural post-workout muscle inflammation and can be used alone for 6 to 10 minutes immediately after a workout.

When you enter the warm water, the blood flows out to your skin and limbs to increase the surface area through which heat can dissipate—just as your skin flushes when exercising in the heat. The cold does the opposite, pulling blood away from the skin and limbs and toward the heart, not unlike what happens when your fingers turn blue in extreme cold. After a workout, this contrast stimulates muscle recovery with little effort.

Hot and cold contrasts force your blood to move fast, from deep in your trunk out to your limbs and skin and then back again. Both playing and training for golf place a significant demand on your body, creating tiny micro tears in muscle fibers that your body repairs in between workouts and leaving your muscles ready to adapt to further training. You don't need access to a hot tub or a cold pool; you can get the same effect in the clubhouse shower by switching between hot and cold settings.

CHAPTER 4 SUMMARY: It's impossible to go all-out all the time. One of the key elements to achieving optimal performance in golf and in life is taking enough time for recovery and regeneration. By taking measures to help your body recover, you'll be better positioned to thrive during your next workout or round of golf. These measures include proper planning, nutrition, sleep, foam roll work and other forms of self-massage, active-isolated stretching, and hot and cold contrasts.

PART 3

CORE PERFORMANCE GOLF NUTRITION

CHAPTER 5

EAT TO PERFORM

You might be surprised to see a section on nutrition in a book about improving golf performance. Perhaps you believe that since you're in fairly decent shape, all you need to do is master the Core Performance movement patterns. You figure that by improving your stability, mobility, and flexibility, you'll be well on the way to enjoying longer drives, lower scores, and pain-free golf.

That's true. But if you skip over this section or fail to apply it, you'll experience only a fraction of the gains you could reap if you followed the entire Core Performance system.

You might think nutrition doesn't matter. Maybe you've gotten along just fine with a little extra weight. Unfortunately, the older you get, the more those surplus pounds take their toll. You're more vulnerable to heart disease and diabetes, you have less energy, and you don't accomplish as much as you otherwise could. I'm sure you know people who can no longer play golf as effectively as they once did as a result of ailments caused by poor nutrition. Perhaps they're in such bad shape that they can't play at all.

No matter how well you're getting along,

I'm sure you'll agree that you could accomplish even more, both on and off the course, if you were in better shape.

Unfortunately, the culture of golf discourages healthy eating. You're out on a course for up to 5 hours and during that time you either don't eat at all, which is not a healthy option, or succumb to junk food, which is even worse. After the round, you retreat to the clubhouse, where the menu tends to be dominated by fried foods and alcohol.

The reason clubhouses offer these foods, other than the fact that they're cheap, highly profitable, easily preserved, and part of the golf culture, is that most golfers prefer to eat this way most of the time. Not only is that bad for your performance on the golf course, it's bad for your long-term health.

In this section, you will learn some nutritional strategies to boost your performance before, during, and after a round. More important, you will learn a simple nutritional framework. This framework will transform your body. You will learn how to eat and drink to fuel your body for optimal energy and production on the golf course, at work, and in every other aspect of life. In short, the Core Performance Golf nutrition plan is an effective way to maximize energy, lose fat, gain lean mass, and save money and time. Before getting started with the program, ask yourself a few questions to get a handle on your current habits:

❯ Have you stocked your pantry, refrigerator, and freezer with foods that you can quickly put together for a nutritious meal or snack any night of the week?

❯ Have you stocked your office, car, and golf bag with similar foods?

❯ Do you ever grab caffeine or snacks at the vending machine to "keep you going" throughout the day?

❯ When you're hungry and searching for your next meal, do you often decide to hit the drive-thru because there isn't enough time to prepare something healthier?

If you answered no to either of the first two questions and yes to either of the last two, you're setting yourself up for long-term health problems. But don't fret—the Core Performance system will help you improve your habits, your physique, and your game.

The purpose behind the questions is to illustrate that at the core of great nutrition are your environment and planning, things as simple as packing your pantry, refrigerator, freezer, golf bag, and desk with nutritious options.

As with the rest of this program, I want you to think not like a golfer but as a golf athlete regarding nutrition. You're competing in a physically and mentally demanding sport, and you need a powerful, turbo-charged body that efficiently burns fuel and produces consistent energy to help you reach your full golf potential.

Eating right can be a challenge—everywhere we turn, someone's trying to sell us quick, convenient, cheap junk food. They will stop at nothing, labeling food "low fat" or "low carb," even as they load it up with harmful sugars and trans fats.

One of the best things you can do to improve your health is to become an educated consumer. Whether ordering a restaurant meal or reading an ingredients label, you need to make the best decision for your healthy lifestyle.

You must also plan and prepare. Otherwise, you're at the mercy of what's out there, and most of it isn't good. The most common reason people eat improperly and sabotage their nutrition programs is shoddy planning.

When it comes to nutrition, like everything else in this program, you have to think long term. It's easy to rationalize eating unhealthy food—after all, you're hungry and you need to eat something. You're not *that* overweight. Perhaps you don't want to be rude to your hosts, refusing a high-fat dish they served. Besides, it really tastes good!

Each time you face such a dilemma, take a step back, as if considering what club to use. Ask why you're on the brink of eating whatever junky food is at hand. Are you letting emotions drive your decisions? Even if you are stuck in a fast-food restaurant or a golf clubhouse with limited options, what's the best choice available?

Remember, those few moments of pleasure junk food provides end quickly. So, too, does the value of the food in terms of producing energy. Soon you'll be hungry again, further contributing to the negative long-term impact that unhealthy food has on your body.

Make a positive investment instead. Each time you eat properly, remind yourself that you're not only giving yourself the energy needed for optimal performance, but investing in your long-term health—to say nothing of helping yourself feel and look better, and play better golf. The reason most diet plans fail is that they tend to address the symptoms—too much weight and lack of energy—rather than the problem, which is poor nutrition in general. But *Core Performance Golf* gets to the root cause by prescribing better choices.

One core element of the program recommends that you eat five or six small meals or snacks a day, which means you get to eat something every 2½ to 3 hours. If you eat often, your body becomes a more efficient energy-producing machine. (Ask yourself what burns more wood, a hot fire or smoldering embers?) Frequent eating also keeps you from overeating. If you know you're going to have something in a few hours, you'll be less likely to overeat—and less likely to be extremely hungry.

Positive thinking, planning, and visualization help your game and help you eat better. Think about all the healthy things you need to eat instead of pining for the things you shouldn't. After all, when you obsess about hooking a shot or landing in the trap, that's often where you end up.

The reason most people don't eat properly is because they don't plan ahead. Here, too, it's necessary to think like a golf athlete, not just like a golfer. If an athlete does not prepare for a match, he's doomed to fail. The same is true with eating—if you don't plan, you end up devouring whatever you can grab.

Stressing out over where and when to eat is unhealthy, a problem made worse by the junk you inevitably consume in such a state. As a result, you end up adding body fat and losing lean mass, which defeats the purpose of following the rest of the Core Performance Golf program. Not only that, but eating on the run is expensive and compromises your health.

As you formulate your game plan, let's first dispel some popular misconceptions.

Eating right is time-consuming. On the contrary, eating right saves time. If you have your meals plotted out for the entire day—or the entire week—you'll save hours each week. Just think, effective planning from following this program might allow you to play an additional round a week. That alone should be sufficient incentive.

Compare the person in your office who brings lunch from home with the person who has to go get takeout. The one who brought lunch from home already has saved a minimum of 15 to 30 minutes, and it's more likely he'll eat a healthier alternative.

I'm not advocating eating at your desk, though in many hectic offices that is inevitable. If that's the case, you'll fall behind by ducking out to locate lunch. Not only that, but if you have lunch handy, you're less likely to go hungry and rush out to find the first option available, which usually is a losing battle. One easy way to get a jumpstart on the week is to do all of your shopping on Saturdays or Sundays, which will help you plan your meals for the week. This is a great way to be proactive about your choices.

Eating right is expensive. Actually, eating right *saves* money. If you've planned your day and week, chances are you'll eat out infrequently, which saves a lot of cash. When you have not prepared ahead of time you're more likely to grab the first option available, regardless of cost.

Why not take that extra money and put it toward greens fees or new equipment?

Let's not forget the greater cost of eating out: the cost to your health. Researchers at the University of Massachusetts found that eating more than one-third of your meals in restaurants increases your risk of obesity by 69 percent.

Eating right means you'll only eat bland, tasteless food. This is a big misconception. It's easy to prepare meals that are healthy and tasty. There are dozens of delicious foods, condiments, and spices that will help you to eat meals that are as delicious as they are good for you.

Fast-food restaurants thrive because they perpetuate these myths. After all, they provide tasty, inexpensive food, quickly. As cheap as such meals are, though, they're still not as inexpensive as meals you planned and prepared yourself. Moreover, low-nutrient, high-sugar, high-fat foods rob you of energy, produce nasty mood swings (and golf swings), and increase body fat. In the long term, they lower your quality of life and overall well-being.

Great performance, whether in golf or in life, begins with the food we eat. No matter how diligently we follow the Core Performance Golf system, it won't matter unless we properly fuel our bodies.

Did you know that most people eat poorly 80 percent of the time? Most of the time, they consume high-calorie foods low in nutrients and fiber. We want to flip that equation, striving to eat *well* at least 80 percent of the time. It's unrealistic to think that we'll be perfect, no matter how hard we plan. Nobody shoots an eagle on every hole. But with a little planning, we can stay under par every time.

It will be tough to improve your performance on the golf course unless you recognize that half of the formula is eating properly. Nutrition not only fuels your body for golf, but it ensures proper recovery. Fueling your body will increase your energy and enhance the quality of your training, enabling you to maximize each of your training sessions and rounds of golf.

Proper diet wards off disease, allowing you to realize the ultimate goal of training: improving your health. Eating right also reduces inflammation that contributes to the muscle pain, joint discomfort, and overuse injuries so common to golf.

You need to view nutrition as your workout partner, an essential tool to optimize your health, training, and performance. So many people view food either with fear ("it will make me fat") or with love ("I live to eat"). Make an effort not to fear your food, nor obsess over it. Instead, you should *eat to live*—look at food objectively, as a potentially powerful means to fuel golf performance.

If you don't give your body the fuel it needs, it becomes catabolic, drawing fuel from and depleting your lean muscle—the very thing you've worked so hard to create. In the catabolic state, muscles are constantly running on fumes. Think of catabolism as shooting back-to-back double bogeys. It negates everything you've accomplished and leaves you scrambling to finish par for the round.

When your body lacks the proper fuel to run or recover, its ability to take on the stress of daily life and training is substantially compromised, and it never has the chance to fully heal. This unbalanced state makes you more susceptible to sickness, fatigue, depression, inflammation, injury, and loss of motivation. It diminishes performance in every way.

Even if you think you're eating properly right now, I guarantee that the following pages will show you ways to eat better and improve performance. Nutrition should be used to enhance your health, your energy, and your performance.

Golf athletes are planners. They're often successful businesspeople who schedule their workdays and time on the course to the minute, but then they may have no idea what they are going to eat for their next meal or snack. Often, I'll ask a golf athlete what he consumes after a round of golf and he'll look at me incredulously. *I eat whatever I want, preferably with beer!*

But that doesn't do you any favors. In short, proper nutrition is the easiest and most effective way to enhance your health and performance. If you do not apply the Core Performance Golf nutrition principles, your progress will be only a fraction of what it would be if you incorporated healthy eating.

Core Performance Golf breaks nutrition down into five simple strategies—a par-5 plan, if you will—along with some advice on what to eat before, during, and after a round. If you can master these strategies, combined with the Core Performance Golf workout program, you'll be in phenomenal shape and in position to play the best golf of your life.

PAR 5 NUTRITION STRATEGY #1:
FUEL UP WITH CARBS

Throughout the 1990s, popular diets conditioned people to believe that carbohydrates must be avoided at all costs. Just as the anti-fat trend of the 1980s indiscriminately gave fats a bad name, carbs were unfairly labeled as the enemy. Thankfully, most people now recognize the importance of carbs to healthful eating.

All food is classified into three nutrient groups—carbs, protein, and fat—and if you neglect any of the three you deprive your body of important nutrients you need to perform at your best. Following a low-carb diet is especially dangerous for athletes, who need carbs to thrive in their sports.

Carbs are our primary source of fuel. They provide energy for muscle function and act as the primary fuel for the brain. When you don't take in enough carbs, your body does not run efficiently or effectively. Think of carbs as the fuel for your body's gas tank. When consumed in the proper amounts, carbs are used for energy and stored in the liver and the muscles for future energy needs. If you eat too many carbs, they will overflow the gas tank and be stored as fat. But if you don't eat enough carbs, you'll run out of fuel during your rounds and workouts, and that will lead to poorer performance.

AVOID THESE HAZARDS
Negative Effects of a Low-Carb Diet

Need more convincing? Eating a low-carb diet is like wringing the water out of a sponge. You'll lose water weight, but as soon as you eat carbs again—and you will at some point, because you need energy to function, and you can only go so long without them—the sponge is going to fill up with water.

Losing water weight is dangerous, especially during a long round of golf on a warm day. For each gram of carbs stored, we also put away 3 grams of water, which is critical to staying hydrated. The easiest way to boost your performance 25 percent—either on the golf course or at the office—is by staying properly hydrated.

You need to fuel your body based on the size of your gas tank. When you follow the Core Performance Golf program, you will require much more fuel than someone who doesn't exercise. Working out regularly burns a lot of fuel and demands a lot of carbs. As your training increases and decreases over the course of a week, month, or year, so should your carbohydrate intake. However, don't lump yourself in with the sedentary and inactive—low-carb diets are not for you!

Not all carbs are created equal, of course: When planning meals, avoid processed carbs such as white breads, pastas, and baked goods. They provide little nutritional value and are converted quickly to sugar and easily stored as fat.

Instead, include fruits, vegetables, and whole grains for their fiber and nutrient density. Your meals should consist mostly of colorful, high-fiber vegetables and grains, which contain powerful vitamins and antioxidants that help to protect the body from the cell-damaging effects of free radicals. If you opt for pasta or couscous, choose the whole wheat option. If you reach for rice, opt for brown or wild rice.

When in doubt, follow the advice of Amanda Carlson, the Director of Performance Nutrition and Research at Athletes' Performance, and "come back to earth." When given a choice between something processed and something more natural, go with the nonprocessed option. Unlike in golf, it's desirable to be "in the rough" when it comes to nutrition. Generally speaking,

The Teaching Pro Says . . .
EAT "IN THE ROUGH"

Here's one instance where being "in the rough" is really important: getting enough fiber. Fiber improves gastrointestinal health and function and helps prevent colon cancer. It regulates blood sugar levels, keeps you full, and promotes long-term cardiovascular health by reducing cholesterol. Fiber is found in oatmeal, beans, whole grains, fruits, and green, leafy vegetables. You can also get it in bottled form—Metamucil products are a terrific source of fiber that you can sprinkle on your meals to improve their nutritional value.

Most people don't get nearly enough fiber in their diet; you need between 25 and 30 grams per day and most people get less than half that amount. When choosing whole grains, look for products that include at least 3 grams of fiber per serving. Because fiber is found mostly in carbohydrates and is essential to overall health, people who follow low-carb diet plans deprive themselves of this vital source of nutrition.

THE GLYCEMIC INDEX

One way to select the best carbs is through the glycemic index, a measure of how a single food will raise your blood glucose level. A food that's highly glycemic will be digested quickly and absorbed immediately, sending your blood sugar level sky-high. The problem is that you crash quickly and end up feeling sluggish.

If you eat the same portion of a low-glycemic food, your body has to work harder to break it down. The benefit is that the sugar from the food will be released into the bloodstream more slowly, giving you steady energy over a longer period.

This is the difference between eating a low-glycemic food, such as asparagus, and a high-glycemic food, such as a doughnut. You already know that the asparagus is better than the doughnut, but it's not just because the asparagus will give you nutrients and the doughnut will add to your midsection. They also have radically different short-term effects on your energy, mood, and performance.

Generally speaking, the lower the number on the glycemic index, the more natural the food will be. Your body has to do the work to extract the nutrients in these foods, and that gradual release helps regulate blood sugar. Look for natural foods that have more color and fiber, since they control appetite, have more nutrients, and improve your cardiovascular health. When you do eat packaged foods, don't worry about memorizing the glycemic index—just look for fiber on the label. If a food has at least 3 grams of fiber, it's a good choice.

By controlling your blood sugar, you're regulating the hormone insulin. If you're constantly jacking up your blood sugar by eating high-glycemic foods, you create a vicious cycle that results in increased calorie consumption and body fat levels, obesity, and perhaps even diabetes.

Glycemic Index of Popular Foods

LOW	MODERATE	HIGH
Sweet potatoes	Mashed potatoes	Baked potatoes
Yams	Sweet corn	Doughnuts
Green peas	Bananas	Waffles
Black beans	Cantaloupe	Bagels
Oatmeal (not instant)	Pineapple	Raisin bran
Peaches	Hamburger buns	Graham crackers
Oranges	Muffins	Pretzels
Apples	Cheese pizza	Corn chips
Grapefruit	Oatmeal cookies	Watermelon

choose slower-digesting carbs during the day and before a workout or round of golf, and include more processed carbs when you need quick energy, such as during or after a round or workouts.

Consuming the recommended amount of carbs each day will ensure that you have optimal fuel stores for training and also help bring your body into balance. So, what quantity of carbs do you need? Don't make the mistake of trying to judge the proper amount of carbs as a percentage of your caloric intake. Instead, go with 1 to 3 grams of carbohydrates per pound of body weight per day. An easy way to measure portion size is to use your fist as a guide. Generally speaking, include a fist-size portion of carbs in your meals.

If you've been cutting back on your carbs, I promise that if you start consuming the proper amount of this crucial nutrient, your performance and energy will improve immediately.

Scorecard:

> Carbs are critical for fueling golf athletes.

> When planning your meals, choose lower-glycemic-index carbs that are rich in fiber. Fist-size portions are a good guideline.

> When selecting breads, cereals, and grains, check the label to make sure the product offers at least 3 grams of dietary fiber per serving.

> If you choose to eat processed, highly glycemic carbs, consume them after a round or training session.

PAR 5 NUTRITION STRATEGY #2: IMPROVE PERFORMANCE WITH PROTEIN

Many people struggle to find the happy medium when it comes to protein. Some people don't get enough, while others follow diets dangerously low on carbs and go overboard on protein.

Protein builds, maintains, and restores muscle. It's responsible for healthy blood cells, key enzymes, and a strong immune system. In order to build muscle, you must consume protein with enough carbohydrate calories to provide your body with energy. Otherwise, your body will tap into the protein for energy. Using protein for energy is inefficient and ineffective for performance.

Just as athletes have higher carbohydrate needs than the average person, they also need more protein. This is especially true of athletes who incorporate strength training into their regimen, as in the Core Performance Golf system.

Exercise produces a catabolic effect, breaking down precious lean body mass. By consuming adequate protein, both throughout the day and especially after rounds and training sessions, we help our bodies minimize and reverse this effect and jump-start our road to recovery.

As a general rule of thumb, you need to consume between 0.6 and 0.8 gram of protein per pound of body weight. If you weigh, say, 180 pounds, you want to shoot for between 108 and 144 grams of protein per day. Generally speaking, the leaner and more active you are, the higher your protein intake should be.

Daily Protein Intake

WEIGHT (LB)	PROTEIN NEEDED (G)
130	78–104
140	84–112
150	90–120
160	96–128
170	102–136
180	108–144
190	114–152
200	120–160
210	126–168
220	132–176

That might sound like a lot of protein—and it is a significant amount—but consider how much protein is in these common foods:

Chicken (4 ounces, skinless, the size of a deck of cards): 35 grams

Cod or salmon (6 ounces): 40 grams

Tuna (6 ounces, packed in water): 40 grams

Lean pork (4 ounces): 35 grams

Lean red meat (4 ounces): 35 grams

Reduced-fat tofu (6 ounces): 30 grams

Cottage cheese (1 cup, 1% or 2% fat): 28 grams

Milk (1 cup of 1%, 2%, or fat-free): 8 grams

One egg: 6 grams

One egg white: 3 grams

Protein intake should be split up over the course of the day, and it should be included in every meal. Protein helps to stabilize energy and also revs up the metabolism. Your body has to work a little harder to digest protein; therefore, your metabolism gets a bit of a jolt each time you include it in a meal. By including a protein source with each of your meals and your post-workout recovery shake, you will easily and effectively satisfy your protein needs.

Here's a good rule of thumb regarding protein: "The less legs, the better." The fewer legs something had when it was alive, the better its ratio of protein to healthy fat.

Fish, for instance, is a healthy source of protein, assuming that it's not fried. Fish such as salmon and albacore tuna also provide an optimal ratio of omega-3 and omega-6 fatty acids. The omega-3 fatty acid helps to promote cardiovascular health and decreases inflammation. Chicken is also a wonderful source of protein, provided the skin is removed and the meat is not fried.

Meat from four-legged creatures can be good, provided it's a lean cut. Lean red meat is a source of important nutrients such as iron and phosphorus. Lean cuts of pork also are good sources of protein.

Low-fat dairy products provide protein, calcium, and vitamin D for strong bones. When you start to consider how much protein

The Teaching Pro Says . . .
PAY ATTENTION TO PRE- AND POST-EXERCISE NUTRITION

You never want your body to be deprived of key nutrients, especially when you work out. Yet many people exercise first thing in the morning on an empty stomach. Although exercising is a great way to start the day, you should eat something before your workout, even if it's just half an apple or a pre-workout "shooter" consisting of a watered-down glass of orange juice with a scoop of whey protein.

Whey is a by-product of cheese manufacturing and includes many essential amino acids that boost the immune system and promote overall good health. It gets into your system quickly, which is especially important prior to or immediately following a workout. I also recommend a post-workout recovery shake, such as Myoplex or Myoplex Lite, produced by EAS. These prepackaged, convenient shakes contain an effective ratio of proteins, carbohydrates, and fat and are loaded with fiber, vitamins, and minerals. Since the shakes can be made by mixing water with a scoop or packet of powder, they make for quick, easy, and portable snacks that won't spoil.

Ideally, you should have a shake right after your workout. At that point, your cells are screaming for nutrients, and drinking one of these shakes expedites the recovery process and maximizes lean-muscle growth. If you had an intense workout, be sure to increase your carbs. Just add a banana or drink 20 ounces of Gatorade in addition to your shake.

Recent research has also shown that a pre-workout shooter may produce an effect equal to a traditional post-workout recovery shake. The pre-workout shooter works its way into the bloodstream to give muscles exactly what they need as quickly as possible.

Because everyone operates under a slightly different schedule, there's no one-size-fits-all routine. But if you remember the priorities—eating often and incorporating a pre-workout shooter and/or a post-workout recovery shake or meal—you can plan your day accordingly.

you really need to eat, you may think it sounds like a lot, but in reality it's a wholly manageable amount.

You should also incorporate a post-workout recovery shake mix into your routine. That mix will contain 20 to 45 grams of protein per serving, along with carbs. If you have one or two shakes a day, along with some combination of poultry and fish for lunch and dinner and a breakfast that includes yogurt or egg whites, you'll easily meet your daily protein goal.

Scorecard:

- ➡ Your body needs significant protein. Make sure you take in between 0.6 and 0.8 gram of protein per pound per day.

- ➡ Include a lean protein source with every meal.

- ➡ A "deck of cards" portion of chicken, lean pork, or lean red meat (about 4 ounces) is equivalent to 35 grams of protein.

PAR 5 NUTRITION STRATEGY #3:
FAT IS NOT THE ENEMY

We need a new word to refer to fat. Thanks to the aggressive anti-fat marketing campaigns of the 1980s, most people believe that if you eat fat, you become fat.

There's some truth to that, of course. Not all fat is good, and too much of anything will contribute to additional body fat. But fats are crucial to good health and the makeup of cell membranes. Fats release energy slowly, keeping the body satiated and regulating blood sugar, thus lowering glycemic response to other foods. Good fats provide powerful nutrients for cellular repair of the joints, organs, skin, and hair. Fats, especially those found in fish oil, also help with cognitive ability, mental clarity, and memory retention, and they have strong anti-inflammatory properties.

Take pains to avoid saturated fats, which are usually found in meat and dairy foods and are solid at room temperature. Saturated fats raise serum cholesterol, clog arteries, and pose a risk to the heart.

The easiest way to avoid saturated fats is to limit your intake of whole-fat dairy products and red meat that's marbled and fatty. The only difference between whole milk and skim products is the saturated fat content. When choosing dairy, go with products labeled 1% or below.

Additionally, stay away from trans fats, which raise bad (LDL) cholesterol but do not raise good (HDL) cholesterol. Artery-clogging trans fats are found in processed foods such as cookies, crackers, pies, pastries, and margarine. They're also found in fried foods and in smaller quantities in meat and some dairy products. Thankfully, food manufacturers must now list trans fat amounts on their product labels.

However, even if the label says "no trans fat," there is a chance there may be some trans fat in the product. If there is less than 0.5 gram of trans fat per serving, the FDA allows the manufacturer to place "no trans fat" onto the package. Yep—the FDA allows the manufacturer to round down. So read the label *and* the ingredients list. If the words "hydrogenated" or "fractionated" appear in any of the first four ingredients, the product likely contains trans fats. If you are choosing minimally processed whole foods, you should not have to worry about trans fats.

The best fats derive from nuts, fish oils, and seeds. Nuts and seeds are a convenient source of protein and fiber, and they stick with you longer than many other snacks, helping to control blood sugar and appetite. Nuts are a convenient on-course snack—a handful every day can lower your risk of heart ailments and Alzheimer's disease and can even lower cholesterol. Nuts and seeds are unsaturated fats, which do not raise cholesterol levels. The best unsaturated fats, liquid at room temperature, are found in olive oil, canola oil, Enova brand oil, and fish oils. Walnuts, in particular, have been linked with decreasing cholesterol and are also a good source of omega-3 fatty acids.

Fish oils also provide powerful omega-3 fatty acids, which have anti-inflammatory properties and are essential for good cardiovascular health and mental clarity. Our bodies need an optimal ratio of omega-6 to omega-3 fatty acids, generally between 4:1 and 10:1 (omega-6 to omega-3). Most diets, though, are typically much higher in omega-6 than omega-3. The omega-3 fatty acids found in salmon, mackerel, lake trout, herring, sardines, tuna, and some types of white fish cannot be made by your body, so they must come from your diet. Unless you eat fish at least three times a week, you're not getting enough omega-3s.

Everyone should have a bottle of fish oil or fish oil capsules in the pantry. Fish oil is high in omega-3 and some omega-6 fatty acids. Blended oils such as Udo's Choice Blend are another good option. Don't sacrifice the health benefits of these oils just because you can't stomach them in liquid form—simply take them as pills. The American Heart Association recommends 1 to 3 grams of fish oil daily. As with any supplement, check with your physician before taking the product.

Scorecard:

➲ "Good" fats are vital for a healthy lifestyle. Examples include fish, olive oil, and nuts.

➲ Choose fats that provide nutritional value, not just empty calories.

- → Avoid trans fats and examine labels carefully.

- → Consider adding supplements such as fish oil to your diet if you do not get the omega-3 you need from food.

PAR 5 NUTRITION STRATEGY #4:
EAT EARLY, OFTEN, AND BALANCED

First and foremost, forget what you've been told about eating three square meals a day and avoiding between-meal snacks. If you want to control your blood sugar level and energy level to improve concentration, regulate your appetite—on and off the course—and build lean body mass, you must eat six small-to-medium-size meals or snacks a day. That means you need to eat, on average, every 3 hours. Think of yourself as "grazing" throughout the day, instead of sitting for three big meals. This is especially important on the golf course. If you can't control your blood sugar levels, you're going to have wild fluctuations in energy levels and compromise your ability to concentrate. Remember this formula: "3 for 3." Eat all three nutrients every 3 hours for optimal energy and body composition.

Like a fire, your metabolism is in constant need of fuel. If you let it go for a long time without adding logs, the fire smolders and dies. Each time you eat (or add fuel) to the fire, it cranks up your metabolism and burns more calories to digest the food. You have an efficient metabolism.

By following the Core Performance Golf program, you'll create this constantly burning fire. If you don't continually fuel the fire, you're going to draw from your valuable lean muscle mass and smolder. If you don't eat often, the most readily available substance for the body to consume is muscle—not fat, as is commonly believed. The body is actually remarkably resistant to fat loss and will turn to lean muscle mass first, keeping that stored fat in reserve as long as possible.

Many people try to stay thin by not eating. They deprive their bodies of nutrients and, while they might look healthy, their bodies may be really out of balance. When your body is not properly nourished, it travels a slippery slope of hormonal imbalance, decreased energy, inability to recover efficiently, and compromised lean muscle mass.

As a golf athlete, you eat to perform. You need to fuel constantly to meet your energy needs and maintain focus, especially on the course. You want to feel great during your training, recover quickly from your sessions, and perform optimally on the golf course and in life. The last thing you want to do is lose the lean mass you've worked so hard to achieve and put your body at a greater risk for injury. Lean mass produces power,

(continued on page 70)

MEAL ASSEMBLY

These days, it's difficult to find time to plan, prepare, and enjoy full meals. That's why I find it valuable to "assemble" meals rather than cook or prepare them.

Prepare for your week on Sunday by grilling a large quantity of chicken, fish, and lean red meat, then cut into individual servings. Steam vegetables and slice tomatoes. Cook plenty of good carbs, such as sweet potatoes, brown rice, couscous, and whole wheat pasta. Grab some prepackaged organic salad mixes and place everything into single-serving containers. That way you'll have plenty of food for the week ahead.

Another easy strategy is to purchase precooked rotisserie chickens, which are widely available and inexpensive. Peel off the skin, pat away the excess oil, cut up the bird, and you'll have enough meat for two to four single meals.

Not only will you have meals to get you through much of the workweek, but you also can put a small cooler in the car for those weekend days when you're out training or running errands. You'll find that it's easy to create a high-performance nutrition plan that is adaptable to any lifestyle and that saves you time and money.

Healthy Meal Components

These tables will help you create healthful meals custom-tailored to your nutritional needs. Make sure you eat your meal or snack within 30 minutes after your workout or round of golf!

GRAINS	PROTEIN		
	MEAT/EGG	DAIRY	VEGETARIAN
1 slice bread (whole wheat optimal) ½ bagel (whole wheat optimal) ½ English muffin 1 whole wheat tortilla (6" size) 1 c high-fiber cereal (such as Kashi) ½ c cooked oatmeal ½ c brown rice ½ c cooked pasta (whole wheat optimal) ½ c cooked whole wheat couscous 1 medium baked sweet potato 1 medium baked potato	4 oz turkey 4 oz skinless chicken 4 oz lean roast beef 4 oz 96% lean ground beef 4 oz lean red meat 4 oz tuna 4 oz salmon or other fish 2 eggs 4 egg whites	½ c cottage cheese 8 oz fat-free or 1% milk 6 oz low-sugar, fat-free yogurt	½ c tofu ½ c cooked beans ½ c soy milk

FRUITS	VEGETABLES	FATS	SUPPLEMENTS*
1 apple 1 banana 1 c berries (fresh or frozen) 1 grapefruit 1 orange 1 peach or nectarine 1½ c grapes 21 cherries 8 strawberries ½–¾ c 100% fruit juice 1 medium fruit ½ c cooked or canned fruit (canned in its own juice)	½ c asparagus ½ c bell pepper ½ c carrots ½ c green beans ½ c mushrooms 1 c spinach (raw or frozen) 1 c romaine lettuce ½ c celery ½ c cooked or raw vegetables 1 c raw leafy vegetables	1 Tbsp olive oil 1 Tbsp flaxseed oil (do not cook with this) ½ avocado ¼ c peanuts, walnuts, or almonds ¼ c low-fat cheese 1 slice low-fat cheese 2 Tbsp low-fat dressing 1 Tbsp regular dressing 1 tsp butter or margarine 1 Tbsp peanut butter 1 Tbsp Enova oil 1 Tbsp fish oil	EAS Myoplex Lite Myoplex Lite RTD *Athletes' Performance exclusively uses EAS products for athlete supplementation because of their banned-substance-free certification from NSF and our strong belief in the efficacy of the products.

Meal Plan for Male Athletes

BREAKFAST	SNACK	LUNCH	SNACK	DINNER	SNACK
3 grains 1 protein 1 fruit 1 fat	1 supple- ment OR 2 grains or fruits and 1 protein	3 grains 2 proteins 1 fat 1 fruit or vegetable	1 supplement OR 2 grains or fruits and 1 protein or fat	3 grains 2 proteins 1 fat 3 vegetables	2 fruits or vegetables and 1 protein or fat OR 1 supplement

Meal Plan for Female Athletes

BREAKFAST	SNACK	LUNCH	SNACK	DINNER	SNACK
2 grains 1 protein 1 fruit 1 fat	1 supple- ment OR 1 grain or fruit and 1 protein	2 grains 1 protein 1 fat 1 fruit or vegetable	1 supplement OR 1 grain or fruit and 1 protein or fat	2 grains 1 protein 1 fat 3 vegetables	1 fruit or vegetable and 1 protein or fat OR 1 supplement

stabilizes joints, promotes movement, and is critical for optimal performance.

The six "meals" are not long, sit-down affairs. (We eat to live, not live to eat, right?) Three of them could be a combination of energy-rich, post-workout recovery shakes, a piece of fruit, a meal replacement bar, or a handful of nuts. Many of these options are nonperishable and can fit in your golf bag.

You could have three moderate-size meals and three small snacks, or you could have six meals of equal size. Your six "meals" will include snacks (mini-meals) and your recovery shake(s). Just remember to make sure that you account for all three nutrients (carbs, protein, and fat) every 3 hours. You should strive for a balance between carbs, proteins, and good fats in each of your meals.

These meals should start early—as soon as you get up. One nutrition cliché that *is* true is that breakfast is the most important meal of the day. Your body has been fasting since you went to bed, so it's important that you "break the fast" not long after rising and keep your body fueled all day long. I can't think of an easier, healthier breakfast than a cup of old-fashioned Quaker Oats and skim milk or yogurt.

I'd rather you eat *anything* for breakfast than skip the meal. When I coached college athletes, I had such difficulty getting them to eat breakfast that I all but begged them to eat leftover pizza instead of going hungry.

That's how important breakfast is, especially if you work out early in the morning—you need to fuel up before training. Research suggests that those who eat before training sessions, a round of golf, or even a challenging day at the office can go harder and longer.

As you build meals through the rest of your day, remember the three nutrients and judge your meals with your visual cues. With a little practice, all you will have to do is look at the plate and you'll know whether it will serve your needs. Typically, your plate should consist mostly of colorful vegetables. There should be a piece of meat or fish the size of a deck of cards and, if you like, a fist-size portion of brown rice or whole wheat pasta. There also should be some "good" fat in the form of something like salmon, nuts, or olive oil.

I recommend that you "eat a rainbow often," which not only refers to the bright colors of fiber-rich fruits and vegetables that should be part of every meal but also reminds you to eat six small meals and snacks a day.

Scorecard:

➲ Think "3 for 3." Eat a combination of carbs, proteins, and fats every 3 hours.

➲ Allowing your body to go long periods without eating contributes to low energy levels, sub-par performance, and breakdown.

→ Consistent fueling throughout the day contributes to increased energy and lean mass.

PAR 5 NUTRITION STRATEGY #5:
WATER IS NOT A HAZARD

We tend to take water for granted. It's readily available, but instead we hydrate with inferior beverages ranging from soda to coffee to alcohol. For all of the advances in technology, we still have not come up with something better than water. It's the perfect beverage.

If I said that you could do up to 25 percent more work or drive a ball 10 percent farther, you'd sprint through a wall to make that happen, right? Actually, it's much easier. Just drink enough water before, during, and after exercise or a round of golf. Try to drink ½ to 1 ounce of water pound of body weight per day. Drink 2 cups of water first thing in the morning. Take a gallon jug to work and drink all day. Keep a bottle in the car.

Proper hydration regulates appetite. A lot of times, people think they're hungry when they're really just thirsty. If you're trying to lose weight, have a glass of water before eating—it will help prevent you from overeating.

If you want to reduce calories quickly, cut them from your drinks. If you replace soft drinks, juices, sports drinks, and beer with water, you'll cut down on calories and sugar. (But stay clear of "speciality waters," which are packed full of sugar and calories. For example, vitamin water has 14 grams of sugar per 8 ounces. Check the labels on everything you drink!) When you reduce calories, your body will burn body fat and high-fiber carbs; you'll lose fat and likely lose weight, too. Always keep a bottle of water close at hand; that way you're more likely to grab water instead of sugary drinks.

Water can also retard the aging process. Because of dehydration, inactivity, and trauma from daily life, the connective tissues around our muscles and joints dry up over time, like chew toys for dogs that start out soft and pliable and end up stiff and brittle. Drinking lots of water prevents this process while improving your muscle tissue and flexibility.

Think of hydration as a means of replacing what you lose when you play golf or work out. Generally speaking, water is all you ever need to get you through a round of golf. But if you're playing in an extremely hot or humid environment, sports drinks that provide carbs, sodium, and potassium are effective. For the times when you need less fuel but all of the fluid and electrolytes, reach for a new Gatorade product called G2.

I'm sure you know the pitfalls of caffeine, alcohol, and soda. Caffeine should not be used as a daily energy source, the way millions of Americans use it. Following the Core Performance Golf workout and nutrition

(continued on page 74)

CORE PERFORMANCE GROCERY LIST

GENERAL SHOPPING TIPS

⊃ **Stay focused.** ⊃ **Go in with a plan.** ⊃ **Avoid products at the heads of the aisles.** ⊃ **Watch out for junk at the checkout counter!** ⊃ **Explore one new healthy food with each shopping trip.**

BAKERY
100% whole wheat bread
(look for fiber)
Pumpernickel bread
Sourdough bread

CEREAL AISLE
Bran cereal
Kashi cereal (my personal favorite)

CANNED FOODS
Black beans
Fruit, packaged, with no sugar
added (canned in its own juice)
Kidney beans
Navy beans
Pinto beans
Tuna, water-packed

DELI SECTION
TIP: Avoid deli salads and fried foods.
Deli meats, lean and reduced-fat
(turkey, chicken, roast beef, ham)
Hummus
Rotisserie chicken (remove
skin and pat off excess oil)

BAKING, SNACK, AND CONDIMENT AISLES
Almonds
Canola oil
Enova oil
High-protein meal-replacement
bars
Mustard
Olive oil
Peanut butter, natural

Peanuts
Low-fat salad dressing
Sunflower seeds
Balsamic or red wine
vinegar for salads

MEAT AND SEAFOOD AISLES
Skinless, white-meat chicken
96% fat-free ground beef
Lean red meat and pork
Salmon and other fish
White-meat turkey

DAIRY SECTION
TIP: Avoid whole-milk products.
Reduced-fat cheese
1% or 2% cottage cheese
100% juice with no sugar added
(look for the same in the frozen
foods and beverages sections)
1% or fat-free milk
Low-fat/low-sugar yogurt

FROZEN FOODS
Fruits
Low-fat/low-sugar ice cream
Kashi waffles
Soy yogurt or ice cream
Vegetables

PRODUCE SECTION
TIPS: Stock up! Cut and package produce to eat later.
Red or green apples
Apricots
Bananas
Blueberries

Broccoli
Carrots
Cauliflower
Cucumber
Edamame
Grapefruit
Red grapes
Green beans
Kiwifruit
Oranges
Pears
Romaine lettuce
Spinach
Strawberries
Sweet potatoes
Tofu
Tomatoes

PHARMACY
Antioxidant complex
Calcium (for women)
Fish oil/omega-3 capsules (Udo's
Choice Blend is one good brand)
Multivitamin
Vitamin C (500 mg)
Vitamin E (400 IU)
Whey protein powder

BEVERAGE AISLES
Regular and decaf coffee
Dry beverages
(such as Crystal Light)
Green, white, and black tea
Bottled water
Red wine

SERVING SIZES

Vegetables: 1 cup raw leafy vegetables, ½ cup cooked or raw vegetables, ¾ cup vegetable juice, ½ cup cooked dry beans

Fruits: 1 medium-size fruit (1 medium apple or medium pear), ½ cup canned or chopped fruit, or ¾ cup fruit juice

Breads and Cereals: 1 slice of bread, 1 cup ready-to-eat cereal, ½ cup cooked rice or pasta

Protein: 4 ounces meat (size of a deck of cards), handful of nuts

Fats: 1 tablespoon olive oil, 1 tablespoon Enova oil, 1 tablespoon flaxseed oil, 1 tablespoon fish oil, 2 tablespoons peanut butter

Dairy: 1 cup milk, ½ cup cottage cheese, 1 ounce or slice of cheese

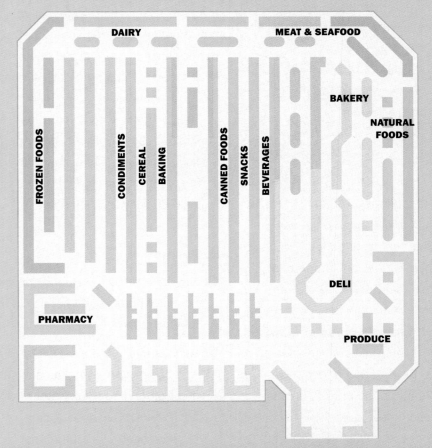

Stay along the perimeter of the store. Avoid the middle aisles, except for the occasional healthy item.

Sports Drinks for Non-Sports Activity

Don't assume that sports drinks are an adequate substitute for water in everyday life. Sports drinks are designed to enhance sport performance. They are not meant to be consumed throughout the day while sitting at your desk or watching television. Many are loaded with high-glycemic carbohydrates that elevate blood sugar and ultimately contribute to body fat if not needed to fuel activity. But when you are golfing in extreme heat, sports drinks are critical for performance.

program means you won't need to rely on stimulants just to get through the day.

Black coffee that isn't loaded with cream and sugar has antioxidant properties, and when consumed in moderation can help meet your antioxidant needs and, of course, increase alertness. For better or for worse, coffee often is the most common source of antioxidants for Americans. However, you should derive antioxidants from a variety of fruits and vegetables (in addition to coffee) and from other drinks such as green, white, or black tea, each of which has different, protective antioxidant properties.

Soda is loaded with sugar or fat-producing high-fructose corn syrup. Did you know that there are roughly 15 spoonfuls of sugar in just one 12-ounce can of soda? Diet soda is better, but it does not offer the same benefits as water.

I also recommend limiting alcohol intake to an occasional glass of red wine, which, according to several studies, reduces the risk of cardiovascular and Alzheimer's disease.

I know it's tough to make these changes. But there's no easier way to maintain consistent energy levels, regulate appetite, boost performance in sports, and improve overall health than to substitute water for soda, coffee, and alcohol.

Always "think before you drink." Are you drinking to stay hydrated, or to produce a certain response? If you substitute water for coffee, soda, and alcohol, you'll have no problem drinking a gallon a day.

Scorecard:

➡ Aim for ½ ounce to 1 ounce of water per pound of body weight per day to maintain hydration.

➡ Think before you drink. Don't hydrate with high-sugar beverages such as soda and fruit drinks. Think water or Gatorade Propel or, if you're golfing in extreme heat, use a performance hydration beverage such as the new Gatorade product G2.

CHAPTER 5 SUMMARY: Even with a hectic schedule, it's possible to eat for optimum health and performance, on and off the golf course. When you follow consistent habits, nutrition becomes second nature. The key is to recognize that nutrition goes a long way toward determining performance and overall health. Good strategies include eating every 3 hours; finding a proper balance of carbs, proteins, and fats; and staying properly hydrated.

CHAPTER 6

TIMING IS EVERYTHING

One concept we use a lot at Athletes' Performance is the "perfect day." The idea is to eat to provide your body with the perfect blend of nutrients over the course of your day. For golf athletes, a perfect day also involves playing at least one round of golf. The challenge is to plan meals properly since you will be on the course for much of the day.

When you're hungry, your blood sugar is down and your brain is looking for nutrients to help you focus on your game. And, if you've eaten nothing but junk food, you're going to have wild fluctuations in blood sugar levels that will affect your mood and focus, which is just as bad as going hungry.

In this chapter you will learn to set yourself up for a great round by eating properly before, during, and after hitting the links.

PRE-ROUND NUTRITION

The morning hours are a great time to play golf. Energy levels are high, courses are less crowded (at least on weekdays), and the heat is less oppressive. Unfortunately, many athletes rush out the door to make an early tee time without eating properly or considering how they'll eat over the course of the day. Not surprisingly, they tend to lose focus by the 12th hole.

If you're playing in the morning, it's essential to eat a balanced breakfast. Failing that, have something—anything—rather than going without. Otherwise you'll be starving, and struggling, by the 5th hole.

Your breakfast should consist of some lower-glycemic carbs, a lean protein source, and some healthy fats. A good example would be egg whites, some low-fat cheese, a cut of fruit, and either two slices of whole wheat toast or a cup of Kashi cereal. Another terrific option would be whole wheat toast and oatmeal, along with some nuts and seeds.

If you play in the afternoon, you've hopefully been eating every 2 to 3 hours all day and are well on your way to a perfect day. But what to eat during the round itself?

IN-ROUND NUTRITION

Golf athletes wouldn't dream of heading out on the course without their equipment. What you take with you to eat and drink is arguably as important as club, ball, or gadget.

In order to maintain the focus necessary to play, you must control your appetite and blood sugar; to do that it's imperative that you stock your golf bag with healthy snacks, just as you would your home, office, and car.

It's an important task, but an easy one: Grab an apple or banana. I also recommend a homemade trail mix consisting of Kashi cereal, nuts, raisins, and dried cranberries or blueberries. Energy bars can be good alternatives, though many are so sugar-laden they might as well be candy bars. I recommend Clif Builder Bars. I also like EAS bars, though they tend to have chocolate, which will likely melt in your bag. Be sure to choose a bar that can survive in the sun for a few hours.

You'll probably want to eat something around the 6th and 12th holes. While the rest of your foursome is going hungry or downing junk food, you're fueling your body for optimum performance. The junk food will wreak havoc with their blood sugar and ability to concentrate, while you'll stay grounded and focused.

Water might be considered a hazard on the golf course, but it's actually an underrated performance weapon. You never want to be dehydrated as it boosts your heart rate and undermines your focus—both are as much your enemies on the course as they are off. Don't wait to come upon a water cooler on the course. Pack in your bag bottled water or a performance hydration drink such as Gatorade or G2.

If you can graze on healthy food throughout the round, you're not only going to be better positioned to play, you'll be less likely to overeat in the clubhouse, where nutritious options are often hard to find.

POST-ROUND NUTRITION

Golf clubhouses are wonderful places to sit back and relive the previous round. Countless business deals have been consummated in clubhouses, and many bright ideas have been drawn up on cocktail napkins in this relaxed atmosphere.

Unfortunately, the clubhouse presents a challenge when it comes to healthy eating. Many golfers feel entitled to eat anything and everything. After all, they just played a grueling round of golf. (What so few take into account is the understanding that if one doesn't fuel properly, as is so often the case, a round of golf will seem considerably more taxing.) But as we've discussed, golf is not a complete game, nor is it much of a workout—it's hardly a license to eat whatever crapola you please. Many people who play the sport are in poor physical condition, and clubhouse menus reflect that.

Now that you're following the Core Performance Golf program on a day-to-day basis, you don't want to fall back into this pattern of unhealthy eating. It's okay to take a day off and treat yourself to something, but wouldn't you rather splurge on something other than chicken fingers and fries?

Assuming you've snacked during both the front and back nines, you won't be famished like your colleagues when you finish your round. The more diligently you follow this system, the less likely you're going to crave battered-fried foods and other clubhouse staples.

At the same time, you will likely be hungry when you leave the course. The key, as with day-to-day eating in the Core Performance system, is to make the best choice. Go with grilled fish or chicken, along with vegetables, and water.

Alcohol is a part of the culture of golf, and this program is meant to complement your lifestyle. I'm not going to tell you to abstain; if I did, you might not comply. All I ask is that you minimize it, and limit yourself to one or two drinks per week. If you're going to have more than that, then I hope you'll have drinks with some health benefit, such as red wines, which have flavonoids that act as antioxidants. (If you drink beer, be sure to factor the carbs into your daily intake.) Always drink one glass of water for every alcoholic drink, as alcohol is a dehydrating diuretic.

CHAPTER 6 SUMMARY: Proper nutrition can go a long way toward fostering great golf. If playing early, be sure to have a healthy breakfast. Stock your golf bag with convenient, healthy snacks that won't melt, and be sure to eat during the round. You'll maintain focus and energy levels and won't overeat in the clubhouse afterward. When eating in golf clubhouses, make the best nutritional choices possible. You can't control a lot of things on the course, but you can control your energy levels and your hydration, both of which will affect your performance.

PART 4

CORE PERFORMANCE
GOLF WORKOUT

CHAPTER 7

CORE PERFORMANCE GOLF WORKOUT: AN INTRODUCTION

I want you to play effective, pain-free golf for as long as you want. If you live to be 100, there's no reason you can't be playing golf right up to your final days.

But the Core Performance Golf program is designed not just to keep you on the golf course. It's meant to keep you active in the game of life. If you don't take action now, the quality of your golf game and your life off the course will deteriorate rapidly.

Even if you're "only" a recreational golfer, your body resembles a professional athlete's, for good and for ill. Unlike much of our increasingly sedentary population, you stay active by playing this wonderful sport. You engage your body and mind on a regular basis. However, because you suffer the effects of golf's repeated one-sided, ballistic movements, you're susceptible to the same injuries faced by golf pros—only you're at greater risk because you take more strokes and probably use a cart.

Playing golf takes a toll, just as surely as sitting at a computer all day has negative consequences, most notably compromised mobility. Joints begin to lock down, and over time, you develop excruciating hip and back problems—ailments exacerbated by golf.

Unless you take action now, you're not only ensuring this decline, you're expediting the process. I have friends between the ages of 35 and 55 who say that it hurts to get in and out of a car. They avoid squatting because it hurts their knees and back. It saddens me because instead of being vibrant, happy, pain-free people, they've aged long before their time.

Research of the aging process suggests that while we might not be able to live decades longer by taking care of our bodies, we can dramatically improve the quality of our remaining years. That's a key part of the Core Performance philosophy: It's not just about the length of time; it's about the *quality* of our time. This program arrests the natural decline of aging, helping you master the fundamental skills you've probably forgotten. We're going to turn on those transmitters that have been shut off due to spending too much time at your desk and not enough on your feet.

It all starts with the notion of activating your core. You want to keep your shoulders relaxed, hanging back and down, and your tummy tight. You also want to initiate movement from your hips and glutes.

If you suffer from back or joint pain, do not exercise regularly (other than playing golf), and possess a lack of energy and muscle tightness, the principles of *Core Performance Golf* will get you out of the rut. These are the same principles applied at Athletes' Performance to improve and prolong the careers of professional athletes.

Most people remain motivated to work out through the teenage and early adult years, if only because they have more time and are looking to impress potential mates. Once you factor a full-time job and family into the equation, it becomes more difficult, but you can—and should—still make the time. Now you have responsibility for someone other than yourself and have even more reasons to want to ensure that you'll be around for a long time.

As the pace of life increases exponentially because of the demands of family, time becomes more precious, and you need an effective and efficient workout solution to maintain the quality of your life, to say nothing of the quality of your golf game. *Core Performance Golf* is that solution.

A common downfall of many fitness programs is a lack of progression: People do the same exercises until their bodies are so used to the program that the exercises no longer confer any benefit. In some cases, as with golf athletes, they've made matters worse by creating muscle imbalances. With

Core Performance Golf, the progression is unlimited. You're not going to be that person in the gym doing the same routine with the same weight at the same time year after year. The more you progress, the more movements you will be able to integrate. You will see greater results, and in less time.

You can customize the workout schedule to fit your needs. You can work out at home with minimal equipment, although on days you golf I highly recommend that you do the workout at the course. On days you don't golf, where the workouts will be a little more involved, you might want to invest in a home gym to save time commuting to the gym. Instead of paying monthly gym fees, take that money and assemble your own Core Performance Golf center at home by visiting www.coreperformance.com and clicking on "Core Store."

We've tested the equipment at Athletes' Performance, and we have added significant value by including educational DVDs with many products to show how you may integrate these tools into the Core Performance Golf program. That allows you to keep mixing things up and progressing using the same effective system.

These versatile, inexpensive pieces of equipment, such as physioballs, medicine balls, foam rolls, and Valslides, don't take up a large amount of space. We've also engineered this system to adapt and grow with your needs.

Recognizing that there will be times when you're limited by a lack of equipment, we've provided options. Here, then, are the five units of the Core Performance Golf workout.

MOVEMENT PREPARATION

Since golf is an endless search for consistency, it inspires most of us to create rituals, whether it's how we address the ball or some of the superstitions we follow over a round. Oddly, though, we give little thought to what transpires *before* the round. Yet, the way we warm up might be the most important factor in achieving a fluid and repeatable swing and establishing mental focus.

One of the signature elements of the Core Performance system is Movement Preparation or Movement Prep, for short. I want you to think of Movement Prep the way a pilot would his preflight checklist. In order to become a world-class golf athlete, your pre-round ritual needs to be upgraded to ensure that every detail of your preflight checklist has been thought out and executed, time and time again. This will become the foundation for you to play consistent, high-level golf. If your warmup is disorganized and inefficient, you'll increase the volatility in your system, and thus the potential for breakdown on the golf course.

Golf athletes recognize that flexibility is a large part of the game, or at least they should. Traditionally, flexibility has been thought of as static stretching. Much like a runner who pushes against a wall or grabs his ankles prior to a race, golfers tend to employ the same stretching routines they learned years ago, usually gripping a club and twisting their backs and shoulders.

Either way, this stretch-and-hold routine is ineffective. The problem with static stretching prior to a round is that it puts muscles in a submissive hold until they shut down. That's the last thing you want and is sure to impede performance in the dynamic and elastic sport of golf.

Movement Prep, which I've used with elite athletes for nearly two decades, is an active series of warmup exercises that efficiently increases the core temperature; lengthens, strengthens, stabilizes, and balances muscles; and, as the name suggests, prepares you for the upcoming movement. It will activate your nervous system so you can maximize your ability to generate consistently high club speed.

With Movement Prep, you're going to both lengthen and strengthen your muscles in the same movement. Movement Prep will reestablish the mobility, coordination, and joint stability you enjoyed in your younger years and improve your strength, balance, and coordination—in other words, it will heighten your body's ability to process information.

You want to improve the long-term mobil-ity and flexibility of your muscles. Rather than have them stretch and revert to where they were—as is the case with stretch-and-hold routines—you want your body to remember these new ranges of motion.

This is done through a process of lengthening the muscle (known as active elongation), which is more effective than a traditional stretch. Here's the crucial difference: After you stretch the muscle through this new range of motion, you stabilize, then contract through the new range of motion. In other words, you don't just stretch your muscles and let them snap back into place, like a rubber band. Instead, you show your muscles how to use the motion.

By adopting the Movement Prep routine, which looks and feels like a combination of golf-specific Pilates and yoga, along with some static stretching, you give your body the ability to create a more natural, fluid swing and swing plane. Golf athletes at Athletes' Performance frequently tell us that after going through Movement Prep for just 5 to 10 minutes before a round, they feel ready to play immediately. No longer do they have to wait until nearly halfway through a round to feel loosened up. I'm sure you can imagine what that means to their performance—and could mean to yours.

Movement Prep might be the most valuable tool you can use to decrease injury, boost performance, improve mobility and stability, and master the movement patterns that are so much a part of golf and life.

The challenge for you is to find somewhere to spend 5 to 10 minutes before a round or practice session to perform the Movement Prep routine. You might feel a little self-conscious doing these exercises, some of which involve touching the ground, moving back and forth, or moving laterally. After all, it's unlikely that anyone else at your club will have adopted the Core Performance Golf program—yet.

I've heard the same reservations from athletes across every sport over the years. Nobody wants to be the first. But that's how champions are made; they're the first to embrace new solutions. These days, if you get to a Major League Baseball game early, you'll see players doing Movement Prep. Athletes everywhere perform it each weekend prior to 10-K races and triathlons. The list of PGA and LPGA stars who do Movement Prep would astound you.

So don't worry about what others think of your pre-round routine. You'll thrive from the first tee while they struggle to loosen up, all the while trying to muster the gumption to ask about your new pre-round routine.

PREHAB

Prehab is not just a few exercises. It's a proactive approach to maintaining your body so that it can meet the demands of the game of life. From your mindset and planning to your nutrition and biomechanics to power and strength exercises to regeneration and everything that happens off the course, Prehab is a common thread that runs throughout this program. Prehab will allow you to play better golf while enjoying better performance off the course.

Prehab is an overall mindset that permeates all aspects of life; our focus, though, is on building your body to withstand golf's demands. The Prehab exercises will isolate and innervate some very specific areas, often with much smaller muscles, so we may integrate them back into more functional movements all the way through your swing. We will target your hips, torso, and shoulders, as well as your lower legs and feet, addressing your mobility, stability, and the efficiency of these muscles and movement patterns.

Unlike "rehab," a reactive process that responds to an injury suffered, Prehab protects your body from backsliding into the pain, inactivity, and dysfunction that lead to the downward spiral. Prehab is a valuable insurance policy. Wherever life and golf take you, Prehab and that meager investment yield considerable results. This routine protects you from shoulder pain, lower-back trouble, hip pain, knee and foot ailments— basically every injury associated with golf. Prehab will give you the necessary balance, coordination, strength, and endurance to function at your best in every respect.

One of the goals of these exercises is to activate your small supporting muscles so that they're turned on and firing properly, and to strengthen them and improve their endurance so they don't wear down over the course of a round or during day-to-day physical activities.

The Prehab unit specifically addresses the rotator cuff, hip cuff, and spine, protecting them all from golf's demanding rotations. Every sport requiring rotational movement—baseball, tennis, hockey, cricket, boxing, basketball—poses these same challenges. In fact, we've yet to find a sport that does not require you to stabilize and move rotationally.

Much of the Prehab unit focuses on rotary stability. During this period, I want your mind to be just as focused as it is when you're putting, worrying about small, precise movements and reading the green. These subtleties in movement patterns and your ability to stabilize—so that the majority of your body remains still while you move some of your limbs—is the difference between shooting a birdie and a double bogey.

Remember that Prehab is not a short-term solution. You will experience immediate results, to be sure, but you must make a long-term commitment. Nothing less than your health and quality of life, on and off the course, is at stake. Remember that the Core Performance Golf mindset transcends your time on the course and permeates your everyday experience.

POWER

Golf has evolved over the last decade because great athletes redefined what's possible with a club and a ball. Golfers are playing a much longer power game, which has even forced the alteration of some of the most storied courses in the world.

This is due in part to advances in technology and equipment. The changes can also be ascribed to the fact that golf athletes have become more *powerful*, not stronger as many golf broadcasters and commentators suggest. Greater power and coordination are manifest in greater and more consistent clubhead speed.

There's a difference between strength and power, but, for our purposes, neither are benefits of long hours in the weight room. We're not looking to build thick, showy muscles. That's not part of the Core Performance program nor a priority for golf athletes. Instead, speed and power are judged relative to the tempo of your swing form—that's where power plays a major role. The swing is not necessarily about strength; it's about the efficient storage and release of elastic energy consistently in your swing plane.

In the Power unit of the Core Performance Golf workout, you will build upon your new foundation of mobility and stability, established through Movement Prep and Prehab, to improve these efficient movement patterns—namely, your body's ability to store and release energy. You won't need space-age workout equipment, but buy that old standby: the medicine ball.

The medicine ball has thousands of years of credibility as a tool to help develop mobility, stability, and power. I love to collect vintage exercise books and it's interesting to see that the medicine ball has had a place in physical development from antiquity to the present day, when we now understand how beneficial training with a medicine ball can be to overall health and fitness.

Despite the medicine ball's long history as an effective training tool, you would have been hard-pressed to find one in national fitness chains just a few years ago. Thankfully, the industry has caught up, and you usually can find a medicine ball, even in smaller hotel gyms.

There are infinite ways to use the med ball, and we're going to start with exercises calling on you to hold the ball as you go through specific movement patterns, accelerating and decelerating the ball as you go. This will help you acquire the ability to store and release elastic energy.

Have you ever wondered why there are wiry golfers who can drive the ball long distances while some bigger, stronger-looking golfers produce only modest drives? It's because elasticity, which translates to power on the golf course, is not a function of muscle size. Elasticity is a function of your ability to store and release energy in a highly coordinated effort within your muscles individually and between them collectively to produce efficient movement. Our goal is to build your body to produce elastic power more efficiently, while protecting it from short-term pain and long-term ailments.

The wiry golfer who can drive the ball tremendous distances has worked to build mobility and stability, which translate into efficient movement patterns for storing and releasing energy. The importance of the athlete's height, weight, and size is negligible. Working with the medicine ball will help you build your mobility and stability so that you too can launch balls deep down the fairway.

The medicine ball is a great teaching tool when it comes to the kinematics of your swing. When you're working on swing mechanics with a light implement like a club, it's possible to overcome bad positioning by using your arms and simply muscling the shot. That overcompensation does not reinforce the proper swing. Worst of all, you might not realize that you've done anything wrong, especially if you're hitting the ball decently.

Unfortunately, this is no way to achieve

the consistency you want, which is why using the med ball is so important and effective. Because of its weight, you'll immediately feel the difference when your body is in a good address position: feet just outside the hips and gripping the ground, knees over your toes, hips sitting up, and back acting as the turret for your "I pillar," feeling tall through your torso and moving in a balanced and fluid way about the center axis.

The medicine ball reinforces a good address position because the ball weighs just enough that if you're slightly out of balance, unstable, or in poor alignment, you'll feel quite awkward and not very powerful. That's a direct biofeedback mechanism that will prompt you to get back in the proper position. Think of your stance when you strike the ball perfectly—the med ball all but forces you to maintain this position, helping to keep you in the ideal address position.

Working with the medicine ball will allow you to master fundamental movement patterns and ensure that you establish important motor function. As you progress, you'll be ready to generate greater power by doing more ballistic throws.

To perform the exercises, find a solid, flat surface, preferably a concrete or block wall. It can be at your health club, at home, on the course—any place where you can throw and catch a medicine ball. Even now, many health clubs do not have a place indoors

that's suitable. You may have to go outside and throw the ball against the building.

At Athletes' Performance, we've become connoisseurs of med balls, and we feature a number of different balls that are more or less likely to bounce. You too will become a med ball aficionado. We recommend you go to the Core Store at www.coreperformance.com or to leading retailers like Dick's Sporting Goods and look for the GoFit med ball, which weighs between 4 and 8 pounds. These balls have been tested and proven at Athletes' Performance to withstand the abuse of being thrown against the wall tens of thousands of times. The GoFit med ball also comes with a complementary DVD of med ball exercises.

Weight is not the only variable involved with the med ball. Like a basketball, a med ball has adjustable air pressure. Early in your med ball training, you'll want to lessen the air pressure so the ball does not rebound as rapidly. This will allow you to master the timing and coordination of the movement. As you get more adept at throwing and catching the ball, increase the air pressure gradually. Greater air pressure boosts the amount of energy the ball will have on the rebound.

When performing these exercises, pay close attention to the position of your hands. Your lead hand—the one closest to the wall—should stay under the ball. Your back hand is perpendicular to the lead hand, and touches it pinkie-to-pinkie. That creates a cup for the ball to sit in and allows you to guide it through the range of motion. To optimize your entire body's contribution to the movement, initiate from your feet and transfer through your hips, torso, shoulders, and into your hands. This will improve kinetic efficiency and develop more power than just throwing the ball with your arms alone.

STRENGTH

Strength is important in golf, but not for the reasons you might think. In the Core Performance Golf program, we talk about two types of strength: stabilizing strength and propulsive strength.

Most people are only familiar with *propulsive* strength and think of it as brute force. Instead, we're going to use strength as the foundation for establishing the motor abilities necessary to improve your performance in golf. Our goal is not to create large muscles, but to help improve muscle efficiency as it relates to your golf game and life.

This unit focuses on multi-joint movements that improve coordination and recruit a number of muscles, a process that expends more energy and gives more return on the time you have invested. It will burn calories and improve balance, stability, flexibility, strength, and the cardiovascular system all at once.

Strength training increases lean body mass, which is the key to a healthy physique. After the age of 25, we lose a pound of lean body mass each year unless we proactively work to reverse that trend. For each pound of extra lean body mass you have, you burn an extra 50 calories a day. Even when you sleep, you'll burn more calories.

It's the difference between a four-cylinder and eight-cylinder engine. Sure, the eight-cylinder requires more fuel, but as we established in the Core Performance Golf nutrition program, a hot fire burns more fuel. You'll eat more often and fuel your body with nothing but the equivalent of premium gas.

Even though the Strength unit is not aerobic exercise, you will get some aerobic benefit from the workout since your heart rate will increase and never fall below a certain aerobic zone. It's as if you're getting an aerobic workout, a two-for-one bonus. It's another example of how you will get the maximum benefit out of your 30 minutes.

By building strength and lean body mass, you'll elevate your metabolism, and that elevated rate will last for a *few days*, as opposed to low-level cardiovascular training, which only gives the metabolism a short-term boost while exercising and in the hours immediately afterward.

Core Performance Golf emphasizes *stabilizing* strength, which supports proper alignment, movement patterns, and energy transfer while helping to reduce injuries and improve performance. In short, the Strength unit acts as a foundation for all movement. The exercises are designed to increase your stabilizing strength, and the plan maximizes your efforts by providing for alternating exercises that work one area while allowing others enough time to recover.

The plan rotates between an "upper body push," an "upper body pull," a "lower body push," and a "lower body pull." The Core Performance Golf program improves your rotary stability, a key component of golf, in every unit of the regimen, protecting you from golf-related and other injuries and maximizing your ability to safely transfer force in golf's rotary movements.

Core Performance Golf also focuses on your posterior chain, or the back side of your body. The posterior chain—hamstrings, glutes, back, posterior shoulders, and neck—is often the most neglected part of your body, perhaps because it's not easy to see in the mirror. The posterior chain suffers a lot of stress from golf, particularly during the address and while putting, and is subject to further stress from everyday activities. The Core Performance Golf program isolates these muscles so that they're working hard in nearly every movement, resulting in improved posture and performance. The movement patterns working your posterior chain will challenge your balance and stability, creating greater mobility.

The Core Performance Golf total-body workout enables you to get more work done in less time and facilitates recovery from each movement pattern, making you feel stronger from set to set. These routines also will increase your heart rate and are adjustable based on both the quality and quantity of your work over each session. This is known as "workout density," meaning that your level of fitness and performance will improve if you boost your total workload during one time frame. Remember that your goal isn't to spend more time working out just better time.

Many of the strength exercises are geared toward increasing your mobility and stability, while improving your coordination and muscular balance. The goal is to continue to create symmetry and balance between the left and right and front and back sides of the body.

If one side of your body or a particular muscle group is too dominant, bad things are bound to happen. I realize that golf is a one-sided sport and that many want only to generate power on the swing side. But what we have seen at Athletes' Performance and what top golf athletes have proven is that the stronger your nondominant side becomes, the greater your potential to store and release energy. Besides increased performance, you will be able to play more golf and get more from the game of life.

The Strength unit requires minimal equipment. You should be able to do this routine at home or on the road. You'll need access either to a cable or to a system such as the GoFit Pro Gym-in-a-Bag, which attaches to the back of any door. It's light, compact, and easy to travel with and store.

You will also use the Valslide, a foot-size slideboard device that improves stability, mobility, and strength. As with everything in the Core Performance system, if you don't have the means to acquire the optimal equipment, you can find simple substitutions around the house. Instead of a Valslide, you can use any slick surface such as hardwood, linoleum, or tile floors. You could even use carpeting if you put one foot over a clipboard or furniture mover—place your foot on the board and slide over the carpet—though the Valslide is compact and travels well. (It comes with an educational DVD.)

Slideboard exercises not only will make you stronger, they'll also release tight muscles. The slideboard leg curl is one of the best all-around exercises for your glutes, hamstrings, calves, and lower back. It also provides an active stretch of the hip flexors and quads. The split and lunge positions that you'll assume are especially useful for stretching the muscles in your hips.

You will use a stability ball to learn specific movement patterns and increase the amount of proprioceptive stimulation in the exercises. Proprioception is the system of pressure sensors in the joints, muscles, and tendons, which provides the body with information to maintain balance. Most people, even top touring pros, do not need any device other than a stability ball to challenge their proprioception. The ball is a versatile piece of equipment that is effective in helping establish these desired movements and coordination patterns.

You probably have access to a pair of dumbbells, either at home or at the golf club. You can purchase a GoFit Sports Block that adjusts from 2 to 24 pounds for just $60.

Nearly every gym has some type of cable and pulley system available. At Athletes' Performance, we exclusively use Keiser, having helped the company design a solution for our athletes that does not rely on mass but on air resistance to allow us to focus on moving at any load, at any speed, and in any movement plane. If you don't have access to a cable system at your gym or at the course, an inexpensive GoFit ProGym is a perfectly effective substitute.

Much like your swing tempo, the tempo of your training is very important. As a general rule of thumb, focus on slowly performing the exercise in two to three counts with an emphasis on more powerful and explosive action during the acceleration part of the movement. This will improve the coordination within and between muscles to generate greater power. And this conscious effort of producing a maximal rate of force development is scientifically proven to generate greater results.

ENERGY SYSTEM DEVELOPMENT (ESD)

Why is cardiovascular conditioning so important for golf athletes? All you're doing is standing over the ball, getting in position, striking, and then hopping in a cart or taking a leisurely walk to the next shot. Unless you're walking uphill, your heart rate should not rise.

Golf athletes resist doing what most people call "cardio" training. I dislike the very term because it's come to mean slow, plodding training that doesn't challenge the body at all. Think of the guy in the gym halfheartedly pedaling on a stationary bike while he watches CNN and talks on his cell phone.

I prefer to use the term *interval training* or Energy System Development (ESD), which my golf athletes often refer to as "extra stuff to do" or "easier said than done." Some of the skinnier ones try to bypass ESD and head for their post-workout recovery shake.

"Extra stuff to digest," they'll say.

Yes, golf athletes have no shortage of reasons to explain why they don't need to do ESD, usually variations on a theme that ESD is irrelevant to the game of golf.

But the fact that ESD is not crucial to golf is precisely the reason why it's so important. Golf is an incomplete game, especially when it comes to challenging your energy level, especially in the modern golf culture. As great a game as golf is, it does not provide vital exercise.

Cardiovascular exercise, and ESD in particular, will dramatically improve your health. It also will improve on-course performance. Successful golf requires prolonged periods of intense focus; by establishing excellent cardiovascular fitness through the Core Performance Golf program, you will regulate blood sugar and energy, ensuring that you have the ability to make great decisions, shot after shot.

The margin for error is small in golf. You never want to take a lousy shot in a fatigued state on the 17th hole, scratch your head and say, "Why did I just do that?" The Core Performance Golf program can help you avoid those blunders: It's one thing to hit a bad shot; it's another thing to hit a bad shot due to a lack of conditioning undermining your potential for success.

When fatigued, it's difficult to concentrate and repeatedly execute the fine motor skills needed in golf. Even though it might not seem like you're exerting a lot of energy in golf, at least relative to some sports, walking and swinging clubs qualifies as physical exertion and can even lead to a spike in heart rate. The more fit you are, the more rapidly your heart rate will descend, returning you to the state in which you've learned and refined your swing mechanics.

Golf is all about repeating the same finely tuned movements. But if your body is accustomed to swinging a club while at a certain heart rate, it's going to be a challenge to execute that same swing after climbing a hill, with your heart racing. You should tackle this issue with as much vigor as you do putting and driving, and recognize that ESD is important and will yield a valuable return on the time invested.

Many people, like that guy in the gym watching CNN, have been doing so-called cardio work for years and experienced little reward. Maybe you're one of those people, even though you've been putting forth decent effort—but now you're in for a change. As it does for the elite athletes that come to our training centers, ESD training will produce rapid improvements in your cardiovascular performance and better utilize the time you're already devoting.

The benefit of the entire Core Performance Golf system is not limited to playing better on the course and feeling better in general. You'll also see a dramatic change in your body, including a reduction of body fat. Some of this will be apparent immediately because of the changes in your posture, but much of the benefit will be derived gradually

from a combination of ESD and the nutrition plan. Even if you haven't lost scale weight, you'll have more lean body mass and people will ask if you've dropped a few pounds. It's just another benefit of being a member of the Core Performance community.

In this unit, we're going to develop each of your energy systems in your body. We'll address short-term conditioning, a powerful system for short bursts employed to develop your lactate system, wherein the greatest opportunity for improvement lies. *Core Performance Golf* will also stimulate overall changes in your aerobic energy system and your body in general.

We've included various interval workouts that change in duration and in intensity, much like the layout of a course. They'll keep you more mentally engaged by alternating short bursts of heavy exertion with easier recovery periods. You should approach interval training much like you do your golf game. In golf, there are intense periods where you stand over the ball and perform your pre-shot ritual, focusing on the upcoming shot. You're totally engaged in the moment, and then you can relax after hitting the ball—assuming it's a good shot.

I want you to have the same mindset as you enter an interval. Make the physical commitment, yes, but also work on your ability to focus on doing the task at hand as well as you possibly can. As soon as that interval is over, make the effort to let your mind and body relax and recover. That way, you'll be able to regain that focus for the next interval, just like you would for the next golf shot.

ESD includes intervals of work and recovery; we call this the work-to-rest ratio. The greater the rest, the higher quality the work should be. The lower the ratio—for instance, 1 second of rest per 1 second of work (1:1)—the bigger the challenge, since the body has less time to recover. That increases your capacity to do work.

With intervals, intensity is more important than volume. You will maintain the same volume—14 to 18 minutes—throughout the program but will ratchet up the intensity as you go along.

The smaller the ratio of work to rest, the more you will improve your body's anaerobic/lactate threshold—its capacity to do high-intensity work. With anaerobic exercise, the body relies more on energy stores than it does on oxygen. It puts you in oxygen debt, which increases the burning sensation in muscles and requires that your body compensate to reduce your heart rate.

Although it can be difficult, there's tremendous benefit to such a plan. It's like tuning a high-performance engine—in this case, the lungs, heart, and related systems. Interval training increases energy production in every cell and in the highways to those cells, allowing you to burn energy more efficiently.

The best part about ESD is that it won't take long. You won't have to jog—or slog—for 3 to 5 miles. This is unproductive for everyone, and counterproductive for golf athletes. The bodies of most have asymmetries and dysfunctional movement patterns. When you add running into the equation, it only compounds the amount of stress on the muscles and joints. There's more aggravation than benefit, both for your health and golf game.

The Core Performance Golf system will correct these bad movement patterns, making your body more efficient, allowing you to do more in a safe and effective manner. You'll focus on longer intervals of walking with very short intervals of high-quality running, using proper mechanics.

Moreover, you can build an effective cardio workout in the gym. Jump aboard a bike, treadmill, elliptical trainer, or VersaClimber and set it on manual so you can control the length of the intervals and intensity. Many of these machines are equipped with heart-rate monitors. You grasp the handles, and within seconds the machine gives you a reading. But just because they're appropriate for the task, don't feel limited to gym machines. Feel free to do your ESD training outdoors, whether it's by taking a hike, scaling stadium stairs, or climbing hills in your neighborhood. One of the great attractions of golf is communing with nature, and if you prefer to be outside doing your ESD work, by all means go for it.

Each ESD workout starts with a warmup period of 3 minutes and alternates intervals of work (30 seconds to 2 minutes) with intervals of recovery (30 seconds to 2 minutes). Do between 1 and 3 repetitions of this interval depending on the stage of the program. There will be a 3-minute cooldown period, which will take you up to a maximum of 18 minutes for each ESD workout.

Par 5 ESD

STAGE	A	B	C	D
WARMUP	3 min	3 min	3 min	3 min
WORK (HARD)	2 min	2 min	1 min	30 sec
RECOVERY (EASY)	2 min	2 min	1 min	30 sec
# OF REPS	3x	3x	6x	8x
COOLDOWN	3 min	3 min	3 min	3 min
TOTAL TIME	18 min	18 min	18 min	14 min

ESD is no time to get sloppy with movement patterns. Regardless of the activity, you should feel tall and stabilized through your pillar. Focus on keeping both feet pointing straight ahead. Fire your glutes and quads, and don't forget to use your arms. You will be amazed at how much more fluid you feel, and at the amount of speed you can maintain with less effort.

Above all, Core Performance Golf ESD prizes a process where your muscles, nervous system, and hormones act together in efficient movement patterns and help your body work as efficiently as possible, instead of doing slow, plodding workouts.

CHAPTER 7 SUMMARY: The Core Performance Golf workout is an integrated program that trains the body for lifelong movement, on and off the course. It consists of six components: Movement Preparation, Prehab, Power, Strength, Energy System Development (ESD), and Regeneration (the last covered in Chapter 4). Movement Prep increases core temperature and lengthens and strengthens muscles for long-term flexibility and stability gains. Prehab is the proactive approach to protecting yourself from injury by building "pillar strength," the integration of shoulder, trunk, and hip stability. Your body needs strength to sustain movement and everyday demands. Power and Strength will enable your body to store and release energy efficiently, which is the key to playing effective golf. Unlike traditional cardio work, ESD focuses on quality, not quantity, and improves the function of your cardiovascular system while building endurance and helping your body create new energy levels.

CORE PERFORMANCE GOLF MOVEMENTS

I realize that you have a hectic schedule. It's tough to find time to actually *play* golf, let alone invest the additional time required by this program to better your game. But by now you've realized that *Core Performance Golf* is essential to playing better golf, and necessary to live a long, pain-free, and vibrant life on and off the course.

The goal with the Core Performance Golf workout is not to keep you in the gym for hours. The goal is to provide you a sizable return on a modest investment of time in the form of better performance on and off the golf course. This is not a quick-fix, 12-week system, but the foundation of your active life.

The Core Performance Golf program work-outs are classified by degree of difficulty as Par 3, Par 4, and Par 5. The Par 3 workout, an abbreviated session designed for days you play, stays consistent throughout the program, while the Par 4 and Par 5 workouts progress as your capacity increases. As you become more proficient with these movements, you'll find you can complete them in less time. In order to keep things challenging, you'll do an additional set or added repetitions, which you'll be able to complete in the original allotted time.

We've also provided additional golf workouts on our Web site, www.coreperformance.com/golf. There, you will find similar exercises that progress by ramping up the movement, changing the proprioceptive demands, or adding a degree of complexity to give you greater return on that particular exercise.

Just as this program leads to greater efficiency, its goal is to provide greater exercise economy as you progress from one level to the next. The Core Performance Golf workout is the long-term performance solution to a time-crunched world. Every other aspect of your life has advanced with technology, enabling you to accomplish more in less time. Why should your workout be any different?

Each workout consists of a few of the following exercise units: Movement Prep, Prehab, Power, Strength, Energy System Development, and Regeneration. Each of these exercises should be completed, ideally, in the specific order in which they're listed on your training plan.

Some days will be more challenging than others. I travel frequently on business, and there are times when it dawns on me that I haven't done anything all day. There's no hotel gym, my room is tiny, and it's nearly time for bed. Even so, it's still possible, and ultimately beneficial, to do some in-room Movement Prep or static stretching before hitting the sack. When demands from family, work, or other obligations knock you off the system, don't worry. That's part of the game of golf and life. What will make you a champion is getting right back up, dusting yourself off, and hopping back into the system.

On days you play a round, you're especially pressed for time. So it's unrealistic to think you're going to be able to complete a Par 4 or Par 5 workout. At the same time, it's especially important on the days you play to invest some time in the Core Performance Golf workout to ensure that you're properly warmed up prior to your first shot. Not only is this important to your golf score, it will go a long way to prevent pain and injuries.

On days you play, you'll do a Par 3 workout that will require just 15 minutes before your round. The workout will consist of 5 minutes of work with an STS Bar, 5 minutes of Movement Prep exercises, and 5 minutes of Prehab movements. Find a place to do this at the course. It can be in the clubhouse, preferably in the workout room, but anywhere you can find some space. It can be near the practice tee, behind the cart shack, or alongside the parking lot.

Golf athletes sometimes ask me if they can do the routine at home. If it's a choice between that and not performing the workout, then by all means do the workout at home; but it's better that you perform the workout at the course prior to the round. When you do the workout at home, you lose some of your momentum on your drive to the course. (Although if you walk to the course, then feel free to perform the workout at home.)

After your round, you'll do 5 minutes of Regeneration. These are exercises to help you jump-start the recovery process. They can be done at the course or at home.

I realize it's impossible to create a one-size-fits-all schedule for golfers. Some play once a week. Some play virtually every day. Try, however, to follow this basic weekly format:

DAY	ODD WEEKS	EVEN WEEKS	ADVANCED
1	Par 4	Par 5	Par 5
2	Off	Off	Par 4
3	Par 5	Par 4	Par 3
4	Par 3	Par 3	Par 5
5	Par 4	Par 5	Par 4
6	Off	Off	Par 3
7	Off	Off	Off

Let's say Day 1 is Monday. The first week, you'll start with a Par 4 workout. On Day 2, Tuesday, take off—unless you plan on playing golf. If that's the case, then do a Par 3 workout as your warmup. If not, take the day off. Do the more challenging Par 5 workout on Wednesday and use Thursday as a

Regeneration day, doing only a Par 3 workout. On Friday, perform the Par 4 workout once again. Saturday and Sunday are listed as "off days," though many people are likely to play golf on one or both of those days. Remember that whenever you play, do the Par 3 workout before hitting the course.

You'll note in the previous chart that there are "Odd Weeks" and "Even Weeks," followed by an advanced program. Start the program by alternating odd and even weeks. If you feel ready for a greater challenge—or have more time—proceed to the advanced level. Now let's take a look at the workouts themselves.

WORKOUT	EXERCISE UNIT	MINUTES
PAR 3	STS Bar	5
	Movement Prep	5
	Prehab	5
	Regeneration	5
PAR 4	Movement Prep	5
	Prehab	15
	Strength	15
	Regeneration	5–10
PAR 5	Movement Prep	5
	Prehab	5
	Power	15
	ESD	15
	Regeneration	10

Par 4 workouts consist of 5 minutes of Movement Prep, 15 minutes of Prehab, 15 minutes of Strength training, and 5 to 10 minutes of Regeneration. Regen can be done either at the end of the workout or later at home. Par 5 workouts consist of 5 minutes of Movement Prep and 5 minutes of Prehab, 15 minutes of Power training, 15 minutes of Energy System Development work, and 10 minutes of Regeneration.

Additional reps and sets are added as you become more proficient with the program in order to keep them challenging. The exercises will not take any additional time, though you will spend just a few minutes more on the ESD portion of the Par 5 workout. You'll know when you're ready to advance a stage when you can perform the exercises perfectly for the prescribed number of repetitions in the allotted amount of time.

There are progressions in each of the workouts, labeled A through D. (See workouts starting on page 196.) When you master Stage D, completing the number of repetitions with perfect form in the allotted time, you can add heavier resistance to make the movements more challenging. Or you can find additional golf workouts at www.coreperformance.com/golf.

Several additional options are also present in the exercise layouts. The first is the Power Plate option. The Power Plate is a revolutionary device that looks like a giant vibrating scale. You simply step on the Power Plate and perform the exercises illustrated in this book. Power Plate's advanced vibration technology stimulates muscle strength and performance and provides a host of other benefits, such as improved flexibility, range of motion, bone density, and blood circulation.

If your golf club has a Power Plate—and they're becoming increasingly common—I encourage you to take advantage of it. Spend just a few minutes performing the exercises specific to the Power Plate in addition to the normal Par 3 workout. (If pressed for time, simply do the Power Plate routine.) You'll be amazed at the results.

I've also provided body-weight exercises for those times when you don't have access to gym equipment but want the benefits of the Par 4 and Par 5 workouts. Finally, there's a brief pre-round Forearm Blast series of exercises that can be performed with a golf club prior to a round. This routine will help prepare this key area of your body for the demands of your round.

CHAPTER 8 SUMMARY: The Core Performance Golf workout is organized into Par 3, Par 4, and Par 5 workout days. The workouts consist of combinations of six exercise units: Movement Prep, Prehab, Power, Strength, ESD, and Regeneration. Do a Par 3 workout on days you play golf and complete a Par 4 or Par 5 workout on other days of the week.

CHAPTER 9

CORE PERFORMANCE GOLF EXERCISES AND WORKOUTS

Before we organize our workouts into Par 3, Par 4, and Par 5 days, let's take a unit-by-unit look at each exercise. Some of these exercises seem awkward or difficult at first, but don't worry—you'll adapt quickly. One of the exciting parts of the Core Performance Golf program is experiencing "aha" moments as you discover new methods of improving performance.

Movement Prep exercises are on pages 106 through 120. You'll find Prehab moves on pages 121 through 130. Strength exercises begin on page 131 and run through page 137. Power moves appear on pages 138 through 142. The Regeneration section runs from page 143 to page 179. The Body-Weight series falls on pages 180 to 187, followed by a Power Plate series on pages 188 to 192. The last grouping of exercises is the Forearm Blast series found on pages 193 to 195.

KNEE HUG—IN PLACE

STARTING POSITION:

Stand with your back straight and your arms at your sides.

PROCEDURE:

Lift your right foot off the ground and squat back and down on your left leg. Grab below the knee with your hands and pull your right knee as close to your chest as you can while contracting your left glute for 1 to 2 seconds. Return to the starting position and repeat on the other side. Continue, alternating sides, for the prescribed number of repetitions.

COACHING KEY:

Keep your chest up. Contract the glute of the leg you are standing on.

YOU SHOULD FEEL:

A stretch in the glute and the hamstring of your front leg and in the hip flexor of your back leg.

INVERTED HAMSTRING STRETCH—IN PLACE

STARTING POSITION:

Stand on one leg with perfect posture, your arms raised out to your sides, your thumbs up, and your shoulder blades back and down.

PROCEDURE:

Keeping a straight line between your ear and ankle, bend over at the waist and elevate your other leg behind you. When you feel a stretch, return to the standing position by contracting the glute and hamstring of your planted leg. Continue with the same leg for the prescribed number of repetitions, then switch legs.

COACHING KEY:

Keep your back flat and your hips parallel to the ground. Maintain a straight line from your ear through your hip, knee, and ankle. Try not to let your foot touch the ground between repetitions.

YOU SHOULD FEEL:

A stretch in your hamstrings.

BACKWARD LUNGE WITH LATERAL FLEXION—IN PLACE

STARTING POSITION:

Stand with your back straight and your arms at your sides.

PROCEDURE:

Step backward with your right foot into the lunge, your left foot forward, then contract your right glute. Reach your right hand overhead and laterally crunch your torso to the left, reaching your left hand toward the ground. Return to the starting position and repeat on the opposite side. Continue, alternating sides, for the desired number of repetitions.

COACHING KEY:

Maintain your posture throughout the movement. Contract your back glute during the stretch. Keep your front knee behind your toes. Don't let your back knee touch the ground. Keep your chest up and fire your front glute as you return to the starting position.

YOU SHOULD FEEL:

Stretching in the hip flexor of your back leg, in the glute and groin area of your front leg, and in the lateral muscles of your torso.

LATERAL SQUAT

STARTING POSITION:

Stand with your feet just outside your shoulders.

PROCEDURE:

Shift your hips to the right and down by bending your right knee and keeping your left leg straight. Your feet should be pointing straight ahead and flat on the ground. Push through your right hip, returning to the starting position. Then shift your hips to the left and down by bending your left knee and keeping your right leg straight. Continue, alternating sides, for the prescribed number of repetitions.

COACHING KEY:

Keep your knee on your "working side" behind your toes. Keep your opposite leg straight, your back flat, and your chest up.

YOU SHOULD FEEL:

A lengthening and stretching of your glutes, groin, hamstrings, and quads.

SEATED ROTATIONS

STARTING POSITION:

From a seated position, squeeze a pad between your knees, or sit straddling a bench.

PROCEDURE:

Place a club behind your back and in front of your elbows. With palms flat on your stomach and maintaining perfect posture without moving your hips, rotate your trunk to the right. Hold for 1 to 2 seconds. Return to the starting position and rotate to the left. Continue, alternating sides, for the prescribed number of repetitions.

COACHING KEY:

Do not let your legs move. Maintain perfect posture throughout. Don't let your hands move from your stomach.

YOU SHOULD FEEL:

A stretch through your torso.

DOWEL SHOULDER STRETCH

STARTING POSITION:

Hold a club with arms extended in front of you, with one palm up, one down, and hands slightly wider than shoulder-width apart.

PROCEDURE:

While maintaining perfect posture, rotate the club so the palm facing up is now facing down and vice versa. Hold the stretch for 1 to 2 seconds, then return to the starting position. Continue for the prescribed number of repetitions. Switch hand positions and repeat on the other side.

COACHING KEY:

Maintain your posture throughout the movement. If you need a bigger stretch, spread your hands farther apart. If you need less, bring your hands closer together.

YOU SHOULD FEEL:

A stretch in your shoulders.

SEATED THORACIC SPINE MOBILITY

STARTING POSITION:

Sit on a bench or on the floor with your hands behind your head and your elbows in line with your ears.

PROCEDURE:

Maintaining perfect posture and keeping your hips still, rotate your trunk to the right as far as possible. At the end of your range of motion, laterally flex your spine, crunching your right elbow down toward the ground. Reverse the crunch and repeat, rotating a bit farther, then crunch your right elbow toward the ground again. Continue for a third repetition and then switch to the other side.

COACHING KEY:

Keep your chest up throughout the movement.

YOU SHOULD FEEL:

Stretching through your trunk and upper back.

HIP CROSSOVER—MODIFIED

STARTING POSITION:

Lie faceup on the ground with your arms to your sides, your knees bent, feet wider than shoulder-width apart, heels on the ground.

PROCEDURE:

Twist your bent legs to the left until they reach the ground, then twist them to the right. Continue, alternating sides, for the prescribed number of repetitions.

COACHING KEY:

Keep your shoulders on the ground and your stomach tight.

YOU SHOULD FEEL:

Stretching through your hips and lower back.

AIS SIDE-LYING SHOULDER STRETCH

STARTING POSITION:

Lie on your side with the upper part of your bottom arm parallel to your belt line and your elbow bent 90 degrees.

PROCEDURE:

Rotate the palm of your bottom hand toward the ground as far as possible, gently pressing your palm farther with the other hand. Hold for 2 seconds, relax, and repeat 10 times. Then switch sides.

COACHING KEY:

Actively try to rotate your palm toward the ground throughout the entire movement. Keep your chin tucked and do not let your bottom shoulder rise off the ground. Start with a small range of motion and gradually increase it.

YOU SHOULD FEEL:

Stretching in your back and the inside of your bottom shoulder.

TENNIS BALL THORACIC SPINE MOBILITY

STARTING POSITION:

Tape two tennis balls together to form a "peanut" shape (see inset right). Lie on your back with the balls under your spine just above your lower back and your hands behind your head.

PROCEDURE:

Perform 5 crunches, then raise your arms over your chest and alternately reach over your head for 5 repetitions with each arm. Move the balls up your spine 1 to 2 inches and repeat the crunches and arm reaches. Continue moving the balls up your spine until they are just above your shoulder blades and below the base of your neck.

COACHING KEY:

During the crunches, try to "hinge" on the ball rather than rolling over it. Think about keeping your ribs pushed down to the ground during the arm reaches.

YOU SHOULD FEEL:

As if you were getting a deep massage in your mid- to upper back.

90/90 STRETCH

STARTING POSITION:

Lie on the ground on your left side in a fetal position, with your legs tucked up to your torso at a 90-degree angle and a pad or rolled-up towel between your knees. Keep both arms straight at a 90-degree angle to your torso.

PROCEDURE:

Keeping your knees together and on the ground and your hips still, rotate your chest and right arm back to the right, trying to put your back on the ground. Exhale and hold for 2 seconds, then return to the starting position. Finish your repetitions, then switch sides and repeat.

COACHING KEY:

Keep your knees together and pressed against the ground. Only rotate as far as you can without lifting or separating your knees. Exhale as you stretch.

YOU SHOULD FEEL:

A stretch through your torso and the muscles of your middle and upper back.

T HIP ROTATIONS

STARTING POSITION:

Stand on your left leg and hold on to a support with your left hand.

PROCEDURE:

Hinge through your left hip by dropping your chest and lifting your right leg to the ceiling to create a perfect "T" with your body. While holding on with your left hand, open your hips and shoulders toward the ceiling until you feel a stretch on the outside of your left hip. Hold for 1 to 2 seconds. Rotate your hips and shoulders down and across your body until you feel a stretch on the outside of your left hip. Continue for the prescribed number of repetitions. Then switch legs.

COACHING KEY:

Move your shoulders and hips as one unit. Keep the leg you're standing on slightly bent at the knee and keep your back leg lifted toward the sky throughout the movement.

YOU SHOULD FEEL:

Stretching on the inside and outside of the hip you're standing on.

LEG CRADLE—IN PLACE

STARTING POSITION:

Stand with your back straight, your knees unlocked, and your arms at your side.

PROCEDURE:

Lift your right foot off the ground and squat back and down on your left leg. Lift your right knee to your chest, placing your right hand under the knee and your left hand under the ankle. Pull your right leg as close as you can to your chest in a gentle stretch while contracting your left glute. Return to the starting position and repeat with your left knee. Continue, alternating legs, for the prescribed number of repetitions.

COACHING KEY:

Keep your chest up. Contract the glute of the leg you are standing on.

YOU SHOULD FEEL:

Stretching on the outside of your hip in your front leg and in the hip flexor of your back leg.

FORWARD LUNGE, ELBOW TO INSTEP—IN PLACE + ROTATION

STARTING POSITION:

Stand with your back straight and your arms at your sides.

PROCEDURE:

Step forward into a lunge with your right foot. Place your left hand on the ground and your right elbow to the inside of your right foot, and hold the stretch for 1 to 2 seconds. Rotate your right arm and chest to the sky as far as you can. Hold for 1 to 2 seconds. Take your elbow back and down toward your instep and reach through to your opposite side. Place your right hand outside your foot and push your hips to the sky. Return your right elbow to the inside of your right foot and repeat for the prescribed number of repetitions on each side.

COACHING KEY:

Keep your back knee off the ground. Contract your back glute during the stretch.

YOU SHOULD FEEL:

A stretch in your groin, your back leg hip flexor, and your front leg glute and hamstring.

QUADRUPED ROCKING

STARTING POSITION:

Get down on all fours with your hands under your shoulders and your knees under your hips.

PROCEDURE:

Pull your belly button in toward your spine while maintaining a natural curve in your lower back. Move your hips backward until you start feeling your pelvis rotating. Return to the starting position and continue for the prescribed number of repetitions.

COACHING KEY:

Draw your belly button in without losing the curve in your lower back or feeling your rib cage expanding. You should be able to breathe normally. Try to hold your pelvis still throughout the range of motion.

YOU SHOULD FEEL:

Compression in the front of your hips. This works your lower back and mobilizes your hips.

MINI-BAND STANDING HIP ROTATIONS

STARTING POSITION:

Stand with your feet slightly wider apart than your shoulders, your hips back and down, your back flat, and a mini band around your legs just above your knees.

PROCEDURE:

Keeping your left leg stationary, move your right knee in and out for the prescribed number of repetitions. Switch legs and repeat.

COACHING KEY:

Keep both feet flat on the ground. Keep your pelvis stable. Don't let the knee of your stationary leg drop in.

YOU SHOULD FEEL IT:

Working your glutes.

FRONT PILLAR BRIDGE—ALTERNATING LEGS

STARTING POSITION:

Lie facedown with your forearms on the ground under your chest.

PROCEDURE:

Push up off your elbows, supporting your weight on your forearms. Tuck your chin so that your head is in line with your body, and pull your toes toward your shins. Lift your left leg into the air and hold for 2 seconds. Place it back on the ground, switch legs, and repeat.

COACHING KEY:

Push your chest as far away from the ground as possible. Keep your belly button drawn in. Keep your head in line with your spine. Don't sag or bend. Do not round off your upper back.

YOU SHOULD FEEL IT:

Working your shoulders and core.

STANDING *Y*s AND *W*s

STARTING POSITION:

Stand bent over at the waist with your back flat and your chest up.

PROCEDURE:

Ys: Hold a golf club, palms up. Glide your shoulder blades back and down, then raise your arms over your head to form a *Y*. Return to the starting position and continue for the prescribed number of repetitions.

Ws: Squeeze your elbows in toward your ribs. Take your thumbs and rotate them back toward the ceiling, squeezing your shoulder blades together to form a *W*. Continue to rotate your hands back as far as possible, keeping your elbows at your sides.

COACHING KEY:

Initiate the movement with your shoulder blades, not your arms. On the *Y*, keep your thumbs up.

YOU SHOULD FEEL IT:

Working your shoulders and upper back.

GLUTE BRIDGE—MARCHING

STARTING POSITION:

Lie faceup on the ground with your arms to your sides, your knees bent, and your heels on the ground.

PROCEDURE:

Lift your hips off the ground until your knees, hips, and shoulders are in a straight line. Hold the position while lifting your right knee to your chest. Return your foot to the ground and repeat with your left knee. Continue for the prescribed number of repetitions.

COACHING KEY:

Do not let your back hyperextend. Do not let your hips drop as your knee comes to your chest.

YOU SHOULD FEEL IT:

Working mainly your glutes, along with your hamstrings and lower back.

STABILITY CHOP—HALF KNEELING

STARTING POSITION:

Half-kneel in an in-line position with your hips perpendicular to a high-cable pulley machine to which you've attached an STS Bar. Your outside knee should be down, and your inside foot should be on the ground. Hold the bar with one hand on each end.

PROCEDURE:

With your shoulders perpendicular to the machine, your chest up, and your stomach tight, let your arms come in toward the machine, with your outside hand low and your inside hand high. Keeping the bar straight, pull your outside hand diagonally down and across your body to the outside shoulder. Then push your inside hand across your body toward the outside shoulder. Return to the starting position and continue for the prescribed number of repetitions. Then face the opposite direction and repeat with the other arm.

COACHING KEY:

Do not allow any movement throughout your trunk during the exercise. Keep your chest up, your shoulder blades back and down, and your stomach tight. Your feet and kneeling knee should be in line.

YOU SHOULD FEEL IT:

Working your shoulders and abdominals.

STABILITY LIFT—HALF KNEELING

STARTING POSITION:

Half-kneel in an in-line position with your hips perpendicular to a low-cable pulley machine to which you've attached an STS Bar. Your inside knee should be down, and your outside foot should be flat on the ground, directly in front of your other knee. Hold the bar with one hand on each end.

PROCEDURE:

With your shoulders perpendicular to the machine, your chest up, and your stomach tight, let your arms come in toward the machine, with your outside hand high and your inside hand low. Keeping the bar straight, pull your outside hand diagonally up and across your body to the outside shoulder. Then lift your inside hand straight up to the ceiling. Return to the starting position and continue for the prescribed number of repetitions. Then face the opposite direction and repeat with the other arm.

COACHING KEY:

Do not let your torso move at all during the movement. Be sure to keep your shoulders perpendicular to the machine. Keep your abs drawn in and your sternum lifted. Your feet and kneeling knee should be in line.

YOU SHOULD FEEL IT:

Working your torso rotators and your upper back, chest, and shoulders.

LATERAL PILLAR BRIDGE

STARTING POSITION:

Lie on your side with your body in a straight line and your elbow under your shoulder, your feet stacked.

PROCEDURE:

Push your hip off the ground, creating a straight line from ankle to shoulder. Hold for the prescribed time. Switch sides and repeat.

COACHING KEY:

Push your torso away from the ground, keeping your tummy tight. Keep your head in line with your spine. Keep your hips pushed forward and your body straight. Maintain straight lines—no sagging or bending.

YOU SHOULD FEEL IT:

Working your shoulders and core.

DIAGONAL ARM LIFT

STARTING POSITION:

Assume a prone pillar bridge with your feet wider than shoulder-width apart.

PROCEDURE:

Without moving your torso, lift your left arm up and slightly to the left and hold for 1 to 2 seconds. Return to the starting position and repeat with your right arm. Continue for the prescribed number of repetitions.

COACHING KEY:

Try to keep your weight even on both feet as your arm lifts. Do not let your trunk move as your arm leaves the ground. Keep your stomach tight throughout the movement.

YOU SHOULD FEEL IT:

Working your shoulders and trunk.

STABILITY PUSH—ADDRESS

STARTING POSITION:

Stand in the address position, with your back to the cable machine set at mid-height, and arms straight in front of you. Your hands should be wider than shoulder-width apart, holding an STS Bar attached to the cable.

PROCEDURE:

Keeping your body still and left arm straight, bring your right hand toward your chest and then return to the starting position. Continue for the prescribed number of repetitions and then switch sides.

COACHING KEY:

Maintain perfect posture throughout the movement. Don't let anything move except your arm.

YOU SHOULD FEEL IT:

In your chest and throughout your torso and hips.

STABILITY PULL—ADDRESS

STARTING POSITION:
Stand in the address position, facing the cable machine set at mid-height, arms straight in front of you. Your hands should be wider than shoulder-width apart, holding an STS Bar attached to the cable.

PROCEDURE:
Keeping your body still and left arm straight, bring your right hand toward your chest and then return to the starting position. Continue for the prescribed number of repetitions and switch sides.

COACHING KEY:
Maintain perfect posture throughout. Don't let anything move except your arm.

YOU SHOULD FEEL IT:
Working your upper back and stabilizing your hips and trunk.

ROMANIAN DEADLIFT—TWO ARMS, ONE LEG

STARTING POSITION:

Stand on one leg holding a pair of dumbbells at your sides. Your leg should be in a fixed position but not locked at the knee. Your weight should be through the middle of your arch with your toes engaged with the ground.

PROCEDURE:

Shift your hips back and lower the dumbbells as far as you can while keeping your back straight. Fire your hamstrings and glutes as you return to an upright position. Continue for the prescribed number of repetitions, then switch legs.

COACHING KEY:

Keep your torso/pillar straight. Keep the dumbbells close to your body, almost touching your legs all the way up and down. Don't think of the exercise as bending forward; think of it as sitting back, but with your torso moving forward instead of staying upright. Keep your shoulder blades back and down throughout the movement.

YOU SHOULD FEEL IT:

In your glutes and hamstrings mostly, with some effort in your lower back and core. You may feel it in your upper back, since it's challenging to keep your shoulder blades retracted as the weight moves toward the ground.

STRENGTH

DUMBBELL BENCH PRESS—ONE ARM

STARTING POSITION:

Lie on a bench, with your left glute and left shoulder blade on the bench and right glute and right shoulder blade off the bench. Hold a dumbbell in your right hand and hold on to the bench with your left hand, above your head.

PROCEDURE:

Slowly lower the weight until your elbow is in line with your shoulder. Return to the starting position. Continue for the prescribed number of repetitions, then switch sides.

COACHING KEY:

Keep your stomach tight and don't let anything move except your arm.

YOU SHOULD FEEL IT:

Working your chest and stabilizing your trunk.

DEADLIFT—ONE ARM, TWO LEGS

STARTING POSITION:

Stand with your feet slightly wider than shoulder-width apart, with a dumbbell on the ground between your legs.

PROCEDURE:

Drop your hips toward the ground until you're in a squat position and grab the dumbbell. Leading with your chest, stand up, and then return to the squat position with the weight on the ground. Continue for the prescribed number of repetitions, then switch sides.

COACHING KEY:

Keep your heels on the ground. Maintain a flat back with your chest up. If you can't hold this position with the dumbbell on the ground, place it on a small box or on several mats (see inset below).

YOU SHOULD FEEL IT:

In your hips and throughout your torso.

ALTERNATING BENT-OVER LATERAL PULL

STRENGTH

STARTING POSITION:

Stand facing a medium-height pulley cable station, holding the cable handles with both hands, palms down.

PROCEDURE:

Keeping your knees slightly bent and your back flat, hinge over at the hips and pull both hands toward your chest. Keeping your torso and left arm still, slowly reach your right hand toward the cable machine and then pull it back to your shoulder. Repeat with your left hand. Continue, alternating hands, for the prescribed number of repetitions.

COACHING KEY:

Keep your back flat and your knees slightly bent throughout the movement. Don't let anything move except the arm that's working.

YOU SHOULD FEEL IT:

Working your hips, torso, and back.

LATERAL CABLE CHOP—HALF KNEELING

STARTING POSITION:

Attach a handle or rope to the high pulley of a cable machine. Kneel on your outside leg on a pad, inside leg up, perpendicular to the machine.

PROCEDURE:

Rotate your shoulders and grab the handle with both hands. Now pull the handle to your chest as you rotate away from the machine, continuing the momentum by pushing the rope down and away. Perform all your repetitions on one side, then repeat on the opposite side.

COACHING KEY:

Turn toward and away from the machine with each repetition. At the end of each rep, your chest should be up, your shoulder blades back and down, and your tummy tight.

YOU SHOULD FEEL IT:

In your shoulders, triceps, and abs.

RUSSIAN TWIST

STARTING POSITION:

Lie faceup on a physioball holding a weight plate, with your shoulder blades on the ball and hips tall.

PROCEDURE:

Keeping your hips tall (see inset below), turn your shoulders to the right so that they're perpendicular to the ground while your hips stay horizontal. Twist back to the starting position and then turn your shoulders to the left side. Continue, alternating sides, for the prescribed number of repetitions.

COACHING KEY:

When rotating to the side, be sure to fire (squeeze) the glute on that side to keep your hips flat.

YOU SHOULD FEEL:

A stretch in your core and an activation of the muscles of your hips and the sides of your waist.

VALSLIDE SPLIT SQUAT

STARTING POSITION:

Stand with one foot on a Valslide (see inset below) or on a slippery surface, such as a file folder or hardwood floor.

PROCEDURE:

Slide your foot backward and drop your hips toward the ground by bending your front knee without letting your back knee touch the ground. Return to the starting position by pushing up with your front leg. Continue for the prescribed number of repetitions, then switch legs.

COACHING KEY:

Do not let your front knee slide forward past your toes or collapse to the inside. Keep your chest up. Keep the glute of your back leg contracted.

YOU SHOULD FEEL IT:

Working your glutes, hamstrings, quads and stretching the hip flexor of your back leg.

MEDICINE BALL LIFT

STARTING POSITION:

Stand holding a medicine ball with two hands.

PROCEDURE:

Squat down while rotating toward your left, holding the medicine ball away from your body. Return to standing by pushing through the ground, then square up and continue to rotate toward your right, pressing the ball over your head and away from your body. Continue for the prescribed number of repetitions.

COACHING KEY:

Keep your chest up and back flat. This exercise combines the familiar movements of squatting, rotating, the upright row, and the incline press. Lower in the same pattern as you lifted.

YOU SHOULD FEEL IT:

In your hips, torso rotators, upper back, chest, and shoulders.

PARALLEL THROW—ADDRESS

STARTING POSITION:

Facing a wall, stand 3 to 4 feet away from it and hold a medicine ball at waist level.

PROCEDURE:

Rotate your trunk away from the wall, taking the ball behind your hip. Initiate the throw by thrusting your hip toward the wall, followed by your trunk, arms, and the ball. With one hand under the ball and the other behind it, catch it with your arms slightly bent. Immediately repeat for the prescribed number of repetitions, then switch sides.

COACHING KEYS:

Keep perfect posture, initiating the throw behind your hip.

YOU SHOULD FEEL IT:

Working your hips and torso.

PERPENDICULAR THROW—ADDRESS

STARTING POSITION:

Stand 3 to 4 feet away from a wall with your hips perpendicular to it and hold a medicine ball in front of your waist, with one hand under and one hand behind the ball.

PROCEDURE:

Rotate your torso away from the wall, taking the ball behind your hip. Initiate the throw by driving your back hip toward the wall, followed by your trunk, arms, and the ball. With one hand under and the other hand behind the ball, catch the ball with your arms slightly bent. Immediately repeat for the prescribed number of repetitions, then switch sides.

COACHING KEY:

Keep your back flat and chest up. Initiate the throw behind your hip.

YOU SHOULD FEEL IT:

Working your hips, torso, and arms.

SQUAT-TO-PRESS THROW

STARTING POSITION:

Stand in an athletic position with your feet shoulder-width apart, holding a medicine ball at chest level.

PROCEDURE:

Sit your hips back and down, keeping your heels on the ground. Reverse the direction by extending through your hips, vertically launching the ball and your body into the air, and throwing the ball straight up and as high as possible. Let the ball bounce to a rest, and then repeat for the prescribed repetitions.

COACHING KEY:

Keep your knees behind your toes and your heels on the ground through the squat descent. Explode and extend through your hips and arms, keeping your chest up.

YOU SHOULD FEEL IT:

Working your hips, legs, and arms.

MEDICINE BALL OVERHEAD PASS

STARTING POSITION:

Stand in an athletic position, with your feet shoulder-width apart and your torso 1 to 2 feet away from a wall, and hold a medicine ball overhead.

PROCEDURE:

Take the ball behind your head and immediately throw the ball into the wall. Catch the ball and immediately repeat for the prescribed number of repetitions.

COACHING KEY:

Maintain perfect posture with your stomach tight. Catch the ball with your hands behind the ball.

YOU SHOULD FEEL IT:

Working the torso, legs, and arms.

FOAM ROLL EXERCISES

Using a foam roll is the next best thing to getting a professional massage. By using one on various body areas as described on the following pages, you'll find that you get much of the benefit, without the cost of a massage therapist.

The more uncomfortable a muscle feels during the foam roll treatment, the more it needs to be massaged. Hold on sore spots for an extended time (30 to 90 seconds) to release them before moving on to the next spot.

FOAM ROLL–CALF

STARTING POSITION:

Sit on the ground with your legs straight, your left leg crossed over the right, and a foam roll under your right calf.

PROCEDURE:

Lift your butt off the ground so that your weight is supported by your hands and the foam roll only. Roll the length of your calf, from your Achilles tendon to behind your knee, and repeat for 30 to 60 seconds per leg.

COACHING KEY:

Place as much weight as possible on the roll. Hold on sore spots for 30 to 60 seconds.

YOU SHOULD FEEL:

As if you were getting a deep massage.

FOAM ROLL–TIBIALIS ANTERIOR

STARTING POSITION:

Get on your hands and knees with a foam roll under the front of your shins, just below your knees.

PROCEDURE:

Keeping your hands still, roll your knees toward your hands, rolling the front of your shins from just below your knees to your ankles. Repeat for 30 to 60 seconds.

COACHING KEY:

Keep your back flat and stomach tight throughout the movement. Place as much weight as possible on the roll. Hold on sore spots for 30 to 60 seconds.

YOU SHOULD FEEL:

As if you were getting a deep massage.

FOAM ROLL–HAMSTRING

STARTING POSITION:

Sit on the ground with a foam roll under the back of one thigh and the other leg crossed over it.

PROCEDURE:

Roll up and down the length of the back of your thigh, for 30 to 60 seconds. Then switch legs and repeat.

COACHING KEY:

If the massage feels too sensitive, uncross your legs and roll both hamstrings at once. Hold on sore spots for 30 to 60 seconds.

YOU SHOULD FEEL:

As if you were getting a deep massage.

FOAM ROLL–QUAD/HIP FLEXOR

STARTING POSITION:

Lie facedown on the ground, supported on your elbows, with a foam roll under one thigh and the other leg crossed at the ankles.

PROCEDURE:

Roll along the quads from your hip to just above your knees for 30 to 60 seconds per leg.

COACHING KEY:

For added benefit, roll slightly on the outside and inside as well as down the front of the thigh. Hold on sore spots for 30 to 60 seconds.

YOU SHOULD FEEL:

As if you were getting a deep massage.

FOAM ROLL–IT (ILIOTIBIAL) BAND

STARTING POSITION:

Lie on your side with a foam roll under the outside of your thigh.

PROCEDURE:

Roll over the foam from your hip to just above your knee.

COACHING KEY:

Hold on sore spots for 30 to 60 seconds.

YOU SHOULD FEEL:

As if you were getting a deep massage.

FOAM ROLL—TFL (TENSOR FASCIAE LATAE)

STARTING POSITION:

Lie facedown, supported on your elbows, with a foam roll under your hip.

PROCEDURE:

Roll along the muscle on the front and slightly to the outside of your upper thigh just below the pelvis for 30 to 60 seconds per leg.

COACHING KEY:

Hold on sore spots for 30 to 60 seconds.

YOU SHOULD FEEL:

As if you were getting a deep massage.

FOAM ROLL–GLUTE

STARTING POSITION:

Sit on the ground with a foam roll slightly below your buttocks.

PROCEDURE:

Roll the back of your thighs to your lower back for 30 to 60 seconds. You might also cross one leg over the other (as pictured below).

COACHING KEY:

Hold on sore spots for 30 to 60 seconds.

YOU SHOULD FEEL:

As if you were getting a deep massage.

FOAM ROLL—LOWER BACK AND QL (QUADRATUS LUMBORUM)

STARTING POSITION:

Lie faceup on the ground with a foam roll under the outside of your midback, just below your rib cage.

PROCEDURE:

Roll from the middle of your back down to your pelvis and repeat for 30 to 60 seconds.

COACHING KEY:

Hold on sore spots for 30 to 60 seconds

YOU SHOULD FEEL:

As if you were getting a deep massage.

FOAM ROLL–MID- AND UPPER BACK

STARTING POSITION:

Lie faceup on the ground with a foam roll under your midback and your head supported with your hands. Keep your elbows together.

PROCEDURE:

Roll from the middle of your back up to your shoulders and repeat for 30 to 60 seconds.

COACHING KEY:

Hold your hands behind your head with your elbows pointed to the sky and close together. Hold on sore spots for 30 to 60 seconds.

YOU SHOULD FEEL:

As if you were getting a deep massage.

FOAM ROLL–CHEST

STARTING POSITION:

Lie facedown on the ground with one arm extended, a foam roll placed under the armpit of the extended arm.

PROCEDURE:

Roll under the arm and over that side of the chest for 30 to 60 seconds. Then switch arms and repeat.

COACHING KEY:

Hold on sore spots for 30 to 60 seconds.

YOU SHOULD FEEL:

As if you were getting a deep massage.

FLEXIBILITY EXERCISES

The following flexibility exercises will help bring balance back to your body. Active-isolated stretching will help lengthen short or stiff muscles by reprogramming your muscles to contract and relax through new ranges of motion. These exercises will help relieve tension throughout your body and alleviate the associated aches and pains. Hold each stretch for 2 seconds while exhaling, then relax and continue for 10 repetitions each.

REACH, ROLL, AND LIFT

STARTING POSITION:

Sit on your heels with your arms extended and the backs of your hands on a foam roll.

PROCEDURE:

Roll the foam forward while keeping your hips back and your chest dropped toward the ground. Lift and exhale as you hold the stretch for 2 seconds. Return to the starting position and repeat.

COACHING KEY:

Attempt to lift your hands off the foam roll as you exhale, but keep your hands in contact with the foam.

YOU SHOULD FEEL:

Stretching in your upper back and shoulders.

AIS BENT-LEG HAMSTRING

STARTING POSITION:

Lie on your back with both legs straight. Pull your right knee to your chest, grasping behind the knee with both hands.

PROCEDURE:

Actively straighten your right knee as much as possible without letting it move away from your chest. Give gentle assistance with your hands until you feel a stretch, hold 2 seconds, and relax. Continue for 10 repetitions, then switch legs and repeat.

COACHING KEY:

Keep your opposite leg on the ground by pushing your heel as far away from your head as possible, contracting your glute. Keep your knee pulled as tightly to your chest as possible throughout the entire movement. It's okay if you can't fully straighten your knee.

YOU SHOULD FEEL:

Stretching in the hamstring of the bent leg and stretching in the hip flexor of the bottom leg.

AIS KNEELING QUAD/HIP FLEXOR

STARTING POSITION:

Half-kneel (put one knee on the ground) with your back knee on a soft mat or pad. Rest your hands on your forward knee.

PROCEDURE:

While keeping a slight forward lean in your torso, tighten your stomach and contract the glute of your back leg. Maintaining this posture, shift your entire body slightly forward. Exhale and hold the stretch for 2 seconds. Relax, repeat 10 times, and then switch legs.

COACHING KEY:

Avoid excessive arching in your lower back.

YOU SHOULD FEEL:

Stretching in the front of your hip and upper thigh of your back leg.

AIS ABDUCTOR

STARTING POSITION:

Lie on your back with both legs straight.

PROCEDURE:

Lift your right knee to your chest, placing your right hand on your knee and your left hand under your ankle. Pull your right leg as close as you can to your chest into a gentle stretch while contracting your left glute. Hold the stretch for 2 seconds, and then relax. Continue for 10 repetitions, then switch legs and repeat.

COACHING KEY:

Throughout the movement, contract the glute of the leg that's on the ground, point that foot toward the ceiling, and keep your belly button drawn in.

YOU SHOULD FEEL:

Stretching in the outside of the thigh of your bent leg.

AIS SUPINE HIP

STARTING POSITION:

Lie faceup on the ground with your arms extended outward, your heels on the ground, and your toes pointed up.

PROCEDURE:

Rotate your hips inward and hold for 2 seconds.

COACHING KEY:

Rotate with your hips, not your knees.

YOU SHOULD FEEL:

A stretch in your hips.

AIS SIDE-LYING SHOULDER STRETCH

STARTING POSITION:

Lie on your side with the upper part of your bottom arm parallel to your belt line and your elbow bent 90 degrees.

PROCEDURE:

Rotate the palm of your bottom hand toward the ground as far as possible, gently pressing your palm farther with the other hand. Hold for 2 seconds, relax, and repeat 10 times. Then switch sides.

COACHING KEY:

Actively try to rotate your palm toward the ground throughout the entire movement. Keep your chin tucked and do not let your bottom shoulder rise off the ground. Start with a small range of motion and gradually increase it.

YOU SHOULD FEEL:

Stretching in your back and the inside of your bottom shoulder.

AIS WRIST FLEXOR

STARTING POSITION:

Stand with your arms slightly extended, palms up, with your right hand on top of your left.

PROCEDURE:

Actively extend your wrist. Grasp the fingers of your right hand with your left hand and gently pull down (see inset below). Hold for 2 seconds and then relax. Continue for 10 repetitions, then switch hands and repeat.

COACHING KEY:

Actively try to extend your wrist throughout the entire movement.

YOU SHOULD FEEL:

A stretch in your wrists.

Trigger point exercises will work similarly to the foam roll; however, with the following exercises it will be much easier to isolate and release deeper tissues. Each one should feel as if you were getting a deep massage. Spend 30 to 60 seconds on each muscle, holding on any sore spots you find for an additional 30 to 60 seconds to release the tissue.

TRIGGER POINT ARCH ROLL

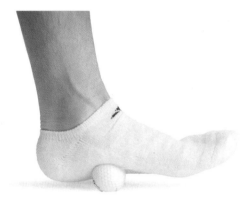

STARTING POSITION:
Stand with your shoes off.

PROCEDURE:
Place one foot on a golf ball or tennis ball. Roll the arch of your foot back and forth over the ball 50 times. Hold on any trigger point for 30 to 90 seconds. Then switch feet and repeat.

COACHING KEY:
The more uncomfortable it is, the more your muscle needs to be massaged. Hold on sore spots for an extended time to release them. Roll through different angles to cover the entire arch of your foot.

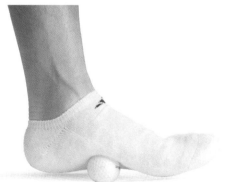

YOU SHOULD FEEL:
As if you were getting a deep massage on the bottom of your foot.

TRIGGER POINT VMO (VASTUS MEDIALIS OBLIQUUS)

STARTING POSITION:

Lie on your stomach with a tennis ball just above your knee (see detail below).

PROCEDURE:

Adjust your position on the ball until you find a sore trigger point. Hold on the spot for 60 to 90 seconds.

COACHING KEY:

Try to maintain as much body weight on the ball as possible. The more uncomfortable it is, the more your muscle needs to be massaged.

YOU SHOULD FEEL:

As if you were getting a deep massage on your VMO.

TRIGGER POINT TFL (TENSOR FASCIAE LATAE)

STARTING POSITION:

Lie facedown, supported on your elbow, with a tennis ball under one hip (see inset below).

PROCEDURE:

Roll the muscle on the front and slightly to the outside of your upper thigh just below the pelvis for 30 to 60 seconds. Switch legs and repeat.

COACHING KEY:

Try to maintain as much body weight on the ball as possible. The more uncomfortable it is, the more your muscle needs to be massaged. Hold on sore spots for 30 to 60 seconds.

YOU SHOULD FEEL:

As if you were getting a deep massage.

TRIGGER POINT GLUTE

STARTING POSITION:

Sit on one hip with a tennis ball under the outside of one of your glutes (see detail below).

PROCEDURE:

Adjust your position on the ball until you find a sore trigger point. Hold on the spot for 60 to 90 seconds. Move the ball to a slightly different spot and repeat.

COACHING KEY:

Try to maintain as much body weight on the ball as possible. The more uncomfortable it is, the more your muscle needs to be massaged. If you experience numbness or tingling in your foot, adjust the ball to a different spot.

YOU SHOULD FEEL:

As if you were getting a deep massage to your glute and piriformis (a muscle in your hip rotator complex).

TRIGGER POINT THORACIC SPINE MOBILITY

STARTING POSITION:

Tape two tennis balls together to form a "peanut" shape (see inset right). Lie on your back with the balls under your spine just above your lower back and your hands behind your head.

PROCEDURE:

Perform 5 crunches, then raise your arms over your chest and alternately reach over your head for 5 repetitions with each arm. Move the balls up your spine 1 to 2 inches and repeat the crunches and arm reaches. Continue moving the balls up your spine until they are just above your shoulder blades and below the base of your neck.

COACHING KEY:

During the crunches, try to "hinge" on the ball rather than rolling over it. Think about keeping your ribs pushed down to the ground during the arm reaches.

YOU SHOULD FEEL:

As if you were getting a deep massage in your mid- to upper back.

TRIGGER POINT NECK

STARTING POSITION:

Lie on your back with a tennis ball just below your neck (see detail below).

PROCEDURE:

Adjust your position on the ball until you find a sore trigger point. Hold on the spot for 60 to 90 seconds.

COACHING KEY:

Try to maintain as much body weight on the ball as possible. The more uncomfortable it is, the more your muscle needs to be massaged.

YOU SHOULD FEEL:

As if you were getting a deep massage in your neck.

Using an STS Bar releases muscle spasms and increases blood and lymphatic flow. Like the foam roll, it's a wonderful self-massage tool. Using the STS Bar is simple; just rapidly roll it over various areas, focusing on sore spots.

STS BAR–FOOT

STARTING POSITION:

Sit on a bench or chair and place one foot on the opposite knee so that an STS Bar can easily reach the bottom of your foot.

PROCEDURE:

As you rub your foot with the STS Bar, look for trigger points—areas that are sore. Massage those areas vigorously for 10 to 15 seconds per trigger point. Spend 30 to 45 seconds on your foot. Then switch feet and repeat.

COACHING KEY:

Maintain steady pressure with the bar throughout the movement.

YOU SHOULD FEEL:

As if you were getting a massage.

STS BAR–CALF

STARTING POSITION:

Stand and place one foot on a bench or chair. Take an STS Bar and hold it behind your calf.

PROCEDURE:

As you rub your calf with the STS Bar, look for trigger points—areas that are sore. Massage those areas with the bar for 10 to 15 seconds. Spend 30 to 45 seconds on your calf, working both inner and outer portions. Then switch legs and repeat.

COACHING KEY:

Maintain steady pressure with the bar throughout the movement.

YOU SHOULD FEEL:

As if you were getting a massage.

STS BAR–PERONEALS

STARTING POSITION:

Stand and place one foot on a bench or stool. Take an STS Bar and hold it along the outside of your lower leg.

PROCEDURE:

As you rub your leg with the STS Bar, look for trigger points—areas that are sore. Massage those areas vigorously for 10 to 15 seconds. Spend 30 to 45 seconds on one leg. Then switch legs and repeat.

COACHING KEY:

Maintain steady pressure with the bar throughout the movement.

YOU SHOULD FEEL:

As if you were getting a massage.

STS BAR–TIBIALIS

STARTING POSITION:

Stand and place one foot on a bench or stool. Take an STS Bar and hold it along the outside of the front of your lower leg.

PROCEDURE:

As you rub your leg with the STS Bar, look for trigger points—areas that are sore. Massage those areas vigorously for 10 to 15 seconds. Spend 30 to 45 seconds on one leg. Then switch legs and repeat.

COACHING KEY:

Maintain steady pressure with the bar throughout the movement.

YOU SHOULD FEEL:

As if you were getting a massage.

STS BAR–HAMSTRING

STARTING POSITION:

Stand and place one foot on a bench or chair. Take an STS Bar and hold it under your thigh.

PROCEDURE:

While rubbing your hamstring with the STS Bar, look for trigger points—areas that are sore. Massage those areas for 10 to 15 seconds. Spend 30 to 45 seconds on your hamstring, working both the inner and outer areas. Then switch legs and repeat.

COACHING KEY:

Maintain steady pressure with the bar throughout the movement.

YOU SHOULD FEEL:

As if you were getting a massage.

STS BAR–QUAD

STARTING POSITION:

Stand and place one foot on a bench or stool. Take an STS Bar and hold it on top of your thigh.

PROCEDURE:

As you rub your thigh with the STS Bar, look for trigger points—areas that are sore. Massage those areas vigorously for 10 to 15 seconds. Spend 30 to 45 seconds on one thigh, working the inner and outer portions. Then switch legs and repeat.

COACHING KEY:

Maintain steady pressure with the bar throughout the movement.

YOU SHOULD FEEL:

As if you were getting a massage.

STS BAR–IT (ILIOTIBIAL) BAND

STARTING POSITION:

Stand and place one foot on a bench or chair. Take an STS Bar and hold it on your outer thigh.

PROCEDURE:

As you rub your IT band with the STS Bar, look for trigger points—areas that are sore. Massage those areas for 10 to 15 seconds. Spend 30 to 45 seconds on your leg. Then switch legs and repeat.

COACHING KEY:

Maintain steady pressure with the bar throughout the movement.

YOU SHOULD FEEL:

As if you were getting a massage.

STS BAR–TFL (TENSOR FASCIAE LATAE)

STARTING POSITION:

Sit on a bench or stool. Take an STS Bar and place it on your outer hip.

PROCEDURE:

As you rub the front and slightly to the outside of your hip with the STS Bar, look for trigger points—areas that are sore. Massage those areas vigorously for 10 to 15 seconds. Spend 30 to 45 seconds on one hip. Then switch legs and repeat.

COACHING KEY:

Maintain steady pressure with the bar throughout the movement.

YOU SHOULD FEEL:

As if you were getting a massage.

STS BAR–GLUTE

STARTING POSITION:

Sit on a bench or stool. Take an STS Bar and hold it on one side of your buttocks.

PROCEDURE:

While rubbing your glute with the STS Bar, look for trigger points—areas that are sore. Massage those areas for 10 to 15 seconds. Spend 30 to 45 seconds on your glute, working up and down the area. Then switch sides and repeat on your other glute.

COACHING KEY:

Maintain steady pressure with the bar throughout the movement.

YOU SHOULD FEEL:

As if you were getting a massage.

STS BAR–LOWER BACK

STARTING POSITION:

Sit on a bench or stool. Take an STS Bar and hold it on your lower back.

PROCEDURE:

As you rub your lower back with the STS Bar, look for trigger points—areas that are sore. Massage those areas for 10 to 15 seconds. Spend 30 to 45 seconds on one side of your lower back and then repeat on the other side.

COACHING KEY:

Maintain steady pressure with the bar throughout the movement.

YOU SHOULD FEEL:

As if you were getting a massage.

STS BAR–MIDBACK

STARTING POSITION:

Sit on a bench or stool. Take an STS Bar and place it along the midpoint of your back, hooking it in the crook of your elbows.

PROCEDURE:

As you rub the midback area with the STS Bar, look for trigger points—areas that are sore. Massage those areas for 10 to 15 seconds. Spend 30 to 45 seconds massaging the entire area.

COACHING KEY:

Maintain steady pressure with the bar throughout the movement.

YOU SHOULD FEEL:

As if you were getting a massage.

STS BAR–UPPER BACK

STARTING POSITION:

Sit on a bench or stool. Take an STS Bar and hold it vertically along your back with one hand over and one hand under.

PROCEDURE:

As you rub across your upper back with the STS Bar, look for trigger points—areas that are sore. Massage those areas vigorously for 10 to 15 seconds. Spend 30 to 45 seconds on one side of your back. Then switch sides and repeat.

COACHING KEY:

Maintain steady pressure with the bar throughout the movement.

YOU SHOULD FEEL:

As if you were getting a massage.

STS BAR–NECK

STARTING POSITION:

Sit on a bench or chair. Take an STS Bar and hold it along one side of the back of your neck.

PROCEDURE:

As you rub your neck with the STS Bar, look for trigger points—areas that are sore. Massage those areas for 10 to 15 seconds. Spend 30 to 45 seconds on one side. Then switch sides and repeat.

COACHING KEY:

Maintain steady pressure with the bar throughout the movement.

YOU SHOULD FEEL:

As if you were getting a massage.

STS BAR–FOREARM

STARTING POSITION:

Sit on a bench or chair and hold an STS Bar vertically, with one end on the bench.

PROCEDURE:

As you rub your forearm with the STS Bar, look for trigger points—areas that are sore. Massage those areas for 10 to 15 seconds. Spend 30 to 45 seconds on your forearm, working both the inner and outer portions. Then switch arms and repeat.

COACHING KEY:

Maintain steady pressure with the bar throughout the movement.

YOU SHOULD FEEL:

As if you were getting a massage.

We all carry with us our own personal set of weights to train with—our body weight. There are many highly effective exercises that use your body weight as resistance. The following body-weight exercises can be performed when you don't have access to a gym or any equipment. They will give you the freedom to train wherever you go. Whether you're traveling on the road or performing a quick workout each morning in your room before you start your day, these body-weight exercises will always be an option for you.

BACKWARD LUNGE WITH LATERAL FLEXION—IN PLACE

STARTING POSITION:

Stand with your back straight and your arms at your sides.

PROCEDURE:

Step backward with your right foot into the lunge, your left foot forward, then contract your right glute. Reach your right hand overhead and laterally crunch your torso to the left, reaching your left hand toward the ground. Return to the starting position and repeat on the opposite side. Continue, alternating sides, for the desired number of repetitions.

COACHING KEY:

Maintain your posture throughout the movement. Contract your back glute during the stretch. Keep your front knee behind your toes. Don't let your back knee touch the ground. Keep your chest up and fire your front glute as you return to the starting position.

YOU SHOULD FEEL IT:

Stretching in the hip flexor of your back leg, in the glute and groin area of your front leg, and in the lateral muscles of your torso.

PUSHUP

STARTING POSITION:

Assume a pushup position.

PROCEDURE:

Lower your body to the ground, then reverse the movement without touching the ground. Keep your body in a straight line. Continue for the prescribed number of repetitions.

COACHING KEY:

Maintain your posture throughout the movement. Keep a straight line through your ankle, hip, shoulder, and ear.

YOU SHOULD FEEL IT:

In your chest, arms, and torso.

INVERTED HAMSTRING STRETCH—IN PLACE

STARTING POSITION:

Stand on one leg with perfect posture, your arms raised out to your sides, your thumbs up, and your shoulder blades back and down.

PROCEDURE:

Keeping a straight line between your ear and ankle, bend over at the waist and elevate your other leg behind you. When you feel a stretch, return to the standing position by contracting the glute and hamstring of your planted leg. Continue with the same leg for the prescribed number of repetitions, then switch legs.

COACHING KEY:

Keep your back flat and your hips parallel to the ground. Maintain a straight line from your ear through your hip, knee, and ankle. Try not to let your foot touch the ground between repetitions.

YOU SHOULD FEEL IT:

Stretching your hamstrings.

STANDING *Y*s AND *W*s

STARTING POSITION:

Stand bent over at the waist with your back flat and your chest up.

PROCEDURE:

Ys: Hold a golf club, palms up. Glide your shoulder blades back and down, then raise your arms over your head to form a *Y*. Return to the starting position and continue for the prescribed number of repetitions.

Ws: Squeeze your elbows in toward your ribs. Take your thumbs and rotate them back toward the ceiling, squeezing your shoulder blades together to form a *W*. Continue to rotate your hands back as far as possible, keeping your elbows at your sides.

COACHING KEY:

Initiate the movement with your shoulder blades, not your arms. On the *Y*, keep your thumbs up.

YOU SHOULD FEEL IT:

Working your shoulders and upper back.

LATERAL SQUAT

STARTING POSITION:

Stand with your feet just outside your shoulders.

PROCEDURE:

Shift your hips to the right and down by bending your right knee and keeping your left leg straight. Your feet should be pointing straight ahead and flat on the ground. Push through your right hip, returning to the starting position. Then shift your hips to the left and down by bending your left knee and keeping your right leg straight. Continue, alternating sides, for the prescribed number of repetitions.

COACHING KEY:

Keep your knee on your "working side" behind your toes. Keep your opposite leg straight, your back flat, and your chest up.

YOU SHOULD FEEL IT:

Lengthening and stretching your glutes, groin, hamstrings, and quads.

DIAGONAL ARM LIFT

STARTING POSITION:

Assume a prone pillar bridge with your feet wider than shoulder-width apart.

PROCEDURE:

Without moving your torso, lift your left arm up and slightly to the left and hold for 1 to 2 seconds. Return to the starting position and repeat with your right arm. Continue for the prescribed number of repetitions.

COACHING KEY:

Try to keep your weight even on both feet as your arm lifts. Do not let your trunk move as your arm leaves the ground. Keep your stomach tight throughout the movement.

YOU SHOULD FEEL IT:

Working your shoulders and trunk.

GLUTE BRIDGE—MARCHING

STARTING POSITION:

Lie faceup on the ground with your arms to your sides, your knees bent, and your heels on the ground.

PROCEDURE:

Lift your hips off the ground until your knees, hips, and shoulders are in a straight line. Hold the position while lifting your right knee to your chest. Return your foot to the ground and repeat with your left knee. Continue for the prescribed number of repetitions.

COACHING KEY:

Do not let your back hyperextend. Do not let your hips drop as your knee comes to your chest.

YOU SHOULD FEEL IT:

Working mainly your glutes, along with your hamstrings and lower back.

LATERAL PILLAR BRIDGE

STARTING POSITION:

Lie on your side with your body in a straight line and your elbow under your shoulder, your feet stacked.

PROCEDURE:

Push your hip off the ground, creating a straight line from ankle to shoulder. Hold for the prescribed time. Switch sides and repeat.

COACHING KEY:

Push your torso away from the ground, keeping your tummy tight. Keep your head in line with your spine. Keep your hips pushed forward and your body straight. Maintain straight lines—no sagging or bending.

YOU SHOULD FEEL IT:

Working your shoulders and core.

POWER PLATE SERIES

The following exercises take advantage of Power Plate's whole-body vibration technology. The Power Plate platform moves in three directions from 30 to 50 times per second allowing the muscles to work in all three planes of natural movement, which stimulates muscle strength and performance. Other benefits of the vibrations are increased circulation, mobility, coordination, and flexibility. It is a terrific training tool for golfers of any age or skill level, and it may become available at more fitness facilities over the next few years.

POWER PLATE T HIP ROTATION

STARTING POSITION:

Stand with your left leg on the Power Plate and hold on to the handle with your left hand.

PROCEDURE:

Hinge through your left hip by dropping your chest and lifting your right leg to the ceiling to create a perfect *T* with your body. While holding on with your left hand, open your hips and shoulders toward the ceiling until you feel a stretch on the inside of your left hip. Hold for 1 to 2 seconds. Rotate your hips and shoulders down and across your body until you feel a stretch on the outside of your left hip. Continue for the prescribed number of repetitions. Then switch sides and repeat.

COACHING KEY:

Move your shoulders and hips as one unit. Keep the knee you're standing on slightly bent and keep your back leg lifted toward the sky throughout the movement.

YOU SHOULD FEEL IT:

Stretching the inside and outside of the hip you're standing on.

POWER PLATE DIAGONAL ARM LIFT

STARTING POSITION:

Assume a pushup position with your feet wider than shoulder-width apart and your hands on the Power Plate.

PROCEDURE:

Without moving your torso, lift your right arm up and slightly to the right and hold for 1 to 2 seconds. Return to the starting position and repeat with your left arm. Continue, alternating arms, for the prescribed number of repetitions.

COACHING KEY:

Try to keep your weight even on both feet as your arm lifts. Do not let your trunk move as your arm leaves the Power Plate. Keep your stomach tight throughout the movement.

YOU SHOULD FEEL IT:

Working your shoulders and trunk.

POWER PLATE GLUTE BRIDGE—ALTERNATING

STARTING POSITION:

Lie faceup on the ground with your arms at your sides, your knees bent, and your heels on the Power Plate.

PROCEDURE:

Lift your hips off the ground until your knees, hips, and shoulders are in a straight line. Hold this position while lifting your right knee to your chest. Return your foot to the Power Plate and repeat with your left knee. Continue, alternating legs, for the prescribed number of repetitions.

COACHING KEY:

Do not hyperextend your back. Do not let your hips drop as your knee comes to your chest.

YOU SHOULD FEEL IT:

Working mainly your glutes and to a lesser degree your hamstrings and lower back.

POWER PLATE QUADRUPED—OPPOSITE HOLD

STARTING POSITION:

Get on your hands and knees on the Power Plate, keeping your belly button drawn in and your shoulders pushed away from the ground.

PROCEDURE:

Lift your right arm and left leg into the air until they are parallel to the ground. Hold for the prescribed amount of time. Return to the starting position and switch sides.

COACHING KEY:

Keep your stomach tight. Do not allow any movement in your trunk throughout the exercise. Only move your arms and legs as far as you can without moving your spine.

YOU SHOULD FEEL IT:

Working your shoulders, back, and stomach.

POWER PLATE QUAD/HIP FLEXOR STRETCH

STARTING POSITION:

Get in a half-kneeling position, with your back knee on the Power Plate and your front foot on the ground.

PROCEDURE:

While keeping a slight forward lean of the torso, tighten your core and contract (squeeze) the glute of your leg with the knee on the ground. Maintaining this posture, shift your entire body slightly forward. Exhale and hold the stretch for 2 seconds. Relax and repeat.

COACHING KEY:

Avoid excessive arching in your lower back.

YOU SHOULD FEEL IT:

Stretching the front of your hip and upper thigh.

The golfer's hand and wrist are the direct link to the club and, therefore, intimately related to the swing and ball strike. The muscles of the forearm take tremendous forces with every swing and can be the weak link with regard to your swing plane and clubhead control as well as wrist or elbow injuries. This quick forearm blast routine can be performed as a warmup at the course or range to make sure you have a solid link between your arm and the club, providing more consistency to your swing while protecting you from injury.

FOREARM RADIAL/ULNAR DEVIATION

STARTING POSITION:

Stand holding an iron in front of your body with your arm at your side and the club pointing to the ground.

PROCEDURE:

Keeping your elbow straight, lift the club forward and toward the sky, moving only at the wrist. Return to the starting position and continue for the prescribed number of repetitions. Switch the club's position so that it points behind your body and then repeat the exercise, moving the club backward.

COACHING KEY:

Keep your elbow straight, moving only at the wrist.

YOU SHOULD FEEL IT:

In your forearm and elbow.

FOREARM PRONATION/SUPINATION

STARTING POSITION:

Stand holding an iron with your elbow bent at 90 degrees.

PROCEDURE:

Keeping your elbow stationary, turn your palm to face the ground. Reverse the direction, turning your palm to the sky. Repeat for the desired number of repetitions.

COACHING KEY:

Keep your elbow stationary. Choke up on the club for decreased difficulty.

YOU SHOULD FEEL IT:

In your forearm and elbow.

FOREARM PRONATION/SUPINATION—REVERSE GRIP

STARTING POSITION:

Stand holding an iron with your elbow bent at 90 degrees.

PROCEDURE:

Keeping your elbow stationary, turn your palm to face the ground. Reverse the direction, turning your palm to the sky. Repeat for the desired number of repetitions.

COACHING KEY:

Keep your elbow stationary. Choke up on the club for decreased difficulty.

YOU SHOULD FEEL IT:

In your forearm and elbow.

PAR 3

STS BAR
(30–45 SECONDS PER BODY PART)

1 FOREARM MASSAGE

2 NECK MASSAGE

3 MIDBACK MASSAGE

MOVEMENT PREP
(5 MINUTES)

STAGE:	A	B	C	D
REPETITIONS:	1 x 3 EA	1 x 3 EA	1 x 3 EA	1 x 3 EA

1 KNEE HUG—IN PLACE

2 INVERTED HAMSTRING STRETCH—IN PLACE

3 LATERAL SQUAT

PREHAB
(5 MINUTES)

STAGE:	A	B	C	D
REPETITIONS:	1 x 8 EA	1 x 8 EA	1 x 8 EA	1 x 8 EA

1 MINI-BAND STANDING HIP ROTATIONS

2 FRONT PILLAR BRIDGE— ALTERNATING LEGS

3 STANDING Ys AND Ws

4 CALF MASSAGE

5 FOOT MASSAGE

6 HAMSTRING MASSAGE

4 BACKWARD LUNGE WITH LATERAL FLEXION—IN PLACE

5 SEATED ROTATIONS

6 DOWEL SHOULDER STRETCH

PAR 4

MOVEMENT PREP (5 MINUTES)

STAGE:	A	B	C	D
REPETITIONS:	1 x 6 EA	1 x 6 EA	1 x 8 EA	1 x 8 EA

1 QUADRUPED ROCKING

2 HIP CROSSOVER— MODIFIED

3 AIS SIDE-LYING SHOULDER STRETCH

PREHAB (15 MINUTES)

STAGE:	A	B	C	D
REPETITIONS:	1 x 6 EA	2 x 6 EA	2 x 8 EA	2 x 10 EA

1 GLUTE BRIDGE— MARCHING

2 STABILITY CHOP— HALF KNEELING

3 STABILITY LIFT— HALF KNEELING

STRENGTH (15 MINUTES)

STAGE:	A	B	C	D
REPETITIONS:	1 x 6 EA	2 x 6 EA	2 x 8 EA	2 x 10 EA

1 ROMANIAN DEADLIFT— TWO ARMS, ONE LEG

2 DUMBBELL BENCH PRESS—ONE ARM

3 DEADLIFT— ONE ARM, TWO LEGS

REGENERATION (5 TO 10 MINUTES) CHOOSE FROM EXERCISES ON PAGES 143 TO 179

4 INVERTED HAMSTRING STRETCH—IN PLACE

5 BACKWARD LUNGE WITH LATERAL FLEXION—IN PLACE

4 FRONT PILLAR BRIDGE—ALTERNATING LEGS

5 LATERAL PILLAR BRIDGE

STAGE:	A	B	C	D
REPETITIONS:	1 x 18 SEC	2 x 18 SEC	2 x 24 SEC	2 x 30 SEC

4 BENT-OVER LATERAL PULL

5 LATERAL CABLE CHOP—HALF KNEELING

6 RUSSIAN TWIST

7 VALSLIDE SPLIT SQUAT

PAR 5

MOVEMENT PREP (5 MINUTES)

STAGE:	A	B	C	D
REPETITIONS:	1 x 6 EA	1 x 6 EA	1 x 8 EA	1 x 8 EA

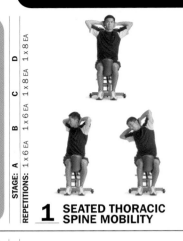

1 SEATED THORACIC SPINE MOBILITY

2 90/90 STRETCH

3 T HIP ROTATIONS

PREHAB (5 MINUTES)

STAGE:	A	B	C	D
REPETITIONS:	1 x 6 EA	2 x 6 EA	2 x 8 EA	2 x 10 EA

1 MINI-BAND STANDING HIP ROTATIONS

2 STABILITY PRESS— ADDRESS

3 STABILITY PULL—ADDRESS

POWER (15 MINUTES)

STAGE:	A	B	C	D
REPETITIONS:	1 x 6 EA	2 x 6 EA	2 x 8 EA	2 x 10 EA

1 MEDICINE BALL LIFT

2 PARALLEL THROW— ADDRESS

3 SQUAT-TO-PRESS THROW

ESD (15 MINUTES) SEE PAGES 94 TO 97

4 LEG CRADLE—IN PLACE

5 FORWARD LUNGE, ELBOW TO INSTEP— IN PLACE + ROTATION

6 LATERAL SQUAT

4 STANDING *Ys* AND *Ws*

4 PERPENDICULAR THROW—ADDRESS

5 MEDICINE BALL OVERHEAD PASS

REGENERATION (10 MINUTES) CHOOSE FROM EXERCISES ON PAGES 143 TO 179

POWER PLATE OPTION

STAGE: A

REPETITIONS: 1–2 x 6 EA

1 POWER PLATE T HIP ROTATION

2 POWER PLATE DIAGONAL ARM LIFT

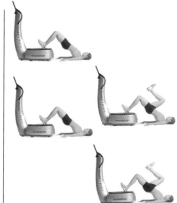

3 POWER PLATE GLUTE BRIDGE—ALTERNATING

BODY-WEIGHT OPTION

STAGE: A

REPETITIONS: 1–2 x 6 EA

1 BACKWARD LUNGE WITH LATERAL FLEXION— IN PLACE

2 PUSHUP

3 INVERTED HAMSTRING STRETCH— IN PLACE

4 STANDING Ys AND Ws

FOREARM BLAST

STAGE: A

REPETITIONS: 1–2 x 10 EA

1 FOREARM RADIAL/ ULNAR DEVIATION

4 **POWER PLATE QUADRUPED —OPPOSITE HOLD**
REPETITIONS: 1–2 x 18 SEC EACH

5 **POWER PLATE QUAD/ HIP FLEXOR STRETCH**

5 **LATERAL SQUAT**

6 **DIAGONAL ARM LIFT**

7 **GLUTE BRIDGE— MARCHING**

8 **LATERAL PILLAR BRIDGE**
REPETITIONS: 1–2 x 18 SEC EA

2 **FOREARM PRONATION/SUPINATION**

3 **FOREARM PRONATION/ SUPINATION—REVERSE GRIP**

AFTERWORD

I n my previous books, I issued a challenge to readers to send us feedback about the program. I've heard from many wonderful folks who have used the Core Performance system to overcome pain, lose weight, increase flexibility, and initiate a plan for high-performance nutrition and exercise for long-term health and success.

I'm especially excited to hear from readers of this book since golf athletes are so process-oriented and will be able to identify in detail how the program has boosted their games. Not only that, golf athletes will be able to quantify their results. So I'll hear about drives increasing by 20 to 30 yards, scores decreasing by 8 to 10 strokes, and perhaps more. Most of all, I'm looking forward to people already passionate about golf telling me how this system has made them enjoy the game even more.

The Core Performance Golf system will help you throughout your golfing life, which can and should last the rest of your days. No longer must you accept a decline in your golf performance as a result of age. With this system, there's no reason you can't get better as you get older. You'll notice that we did not put a time frame on this program. There's no "12 Weeks to a Longer Drive" slogan, no "Better Golf in 30 Days" subtitle. Your game is limitless.

Core Performance is not just a workout

routine. By picking up this book, you have entered into the Core Performance community, which allows you to benefit from the core values and fundamentals to perform in golf and in the game of life. Books are a terrific medium to share thoughts and ideas to help readers improve the quality of their lives, and that's been the goal of *Core Performance Golf.*

GOLF/GAME OF LIFE

IN

PERFORM

TO

CORE FUNDAMENTALS
MINDSET. NUTRITION. MOVEMENT. RECOVERY.

For additional information, you might find one of our previous books, *Core Performance Essentials* (now in paperback), helpful in laying out more general strategies that you can easily employ in your own home. If you want to dial up your training a notch or two, our original *Core Performance* book (also in paperback) definitely will keep you challenged.

Many of our readers have found it useful to watch DVDs of our workouts as a reminder and a useful aid in performing the exercises properly. We have specific DVD products for golf and other sports, along with the general Core Performance system, available at our Web site (www.coreperformance.com), as

well as at retail stores such as Dick's Sporting Goods, Target, and most other national specialty chains via our industry-leading partner, GoFit.

We hope you'll continue to reference this book throughout your golf career. At the same time, we want to be a trusted resource for you to cut through the marketing and health-and-fitness information clutter bombarding you every day. We want to provide you with the best ongoing strategies to upgrade your mindset, nutrition, movement, and recovery to help build and sustain energy in golf and in life. We realize that your game of life will continually evolve, and we'll be here to offer you solutions and advice. It's a two-way street; we want to hear from and work with you on these solutions.

The platform for this is our Web site, www.coreperformance.com/golf. Here you'll find interactive content to help you perform, whether you're serious about golf or just improving your life generally. Here you can create an individualized "perfect day" game plan that includes nutrition and a customized workout, whether it's for golf, another sport, or just your daily demands. This will allow you to truly customize the experience, from the moment you wake up to when you go to bed. You can budget how much time you work out and on what days, while planning how you will accomplish your loftiest goals. It doesn't matter if you have not exercised in years or you are a serious athlete, you will find solutions waiting for you at www.coreperformance.com/golf.

Here you can ask questions of our team of experts from Athletes' Performance. This book does not (and cannot) provide all the answers, but it is one resource that will help you begin your path to better golf and a better life; meanwhile, the Web site will be there for you as your life and interests evolve.

Coreperformance.com gives you access to a wealth of free content and individualized training programs, and it is your gateway to our online Core Store. At the Core Store, we have assembled several packages to create a Core Performance Golf Center in a corner of your home. I know that you are incredibly busy, and maybe a gym membership is just not feasible, or maybe you have a membership but are never able to use it. A simple Core Performance Center home gym lets you structure Core Performance around *your* life.

Maybe you're thinking, "Sure, that would be great, but I don't have the time or space for elaborate equipment." The beauty of this is that the equipment is easy to use and compact. It will fit under your bed or in a small corner of a room.

GoFit, our official equipment partner, has teamed with us to compile several affordable packages of equipment that you can purchase in the Core Store. Of course, you also can purchase individual pieces of equipment to fit your needs.

All of the products you'll find online are tested and used at Athletes' Performance by the top champions in sport. The Core Store also provides educational DVDs, which will expand on the information in this book, giving you additional levels and progressions of exercises.

Ultimately, I want you to be members of the Core Performance online community for life, which is why we have made a membership available for less than the cost of a weekly cup of coffee. This means that for the cost of a personal training session, you will have progressive programs based upon your lifestyle and accomplishments that evolve with you as your goals and needs change.

I've had great success supporting people in the pursuit of their dreams, from prominent sports figures to readers who have reached spectacular goals. What I love most is being able to build my athletes, to see them evolve and reach their goals in sport and in the game of life.

Ultimately, you are responsible for your performance. That's why I love the mindset of golf athletes like you. You realize that in golf, you alone are responsible and accountable for your performance. No one else can go out and shoot a round for you, and no one else can hold you accountable to integrate these proven systems to attain your goals.

I want to hear how this program has transformed your game—and not just on the course. Tell me how it's enabled you to meet challenges, overcome injuries, and fulfill your dreams. Tell the entire Core Performance community how taking a proactive approach to life has transcended the golf course and enabled you to make a difference.

Please share your stories with us: Write us at success@coreperformance.com. We'll pick the most inspirational submissions, the ones that touch us the most, and bring the authors of those remarks to Athletes' Performance to train in person with our staff, alongside some of the best athletes in the world.

We can't bring everyone out, unfortunately. I hope you join our online community and interact with the growing number of people dedicated to treating each day as an athletic event and properly preparing themselves for the competition that is the game of life.

You now have the resources to achieve your goals on and off the course. We've done our part and we will continue to be there for you every day at coreperformance.com. I expect you to hold up your end of the relationship and move toward your goals on a daily basis. All of us here in the Core Performance community are honored to be working with you.

Welcome to the exclusive golf community of Core Performance.

Your coach,

Mark Verstegen

FREQUENTLY ASKED QUESTIONS (FAQs)

Q: **I get regular massages. Won't that solve most of the golf-related muscle imbalances and asymmetries you discuss in the book?**

A: Rubdowns from a licensed massage therapist are valuable to those who can afford them. A massage therapist will release tight tissue; some are even qualified to make structural fascial changes. But massage therapy is only part of the equation. We need to use the Core Performance Golf program to create long-term mobility and stability and more efficient movement patterns. That way, spasms and tightness won't reoccur, making your life, and that of your therapist, much easier!

Q: **I do yoga and Pilates. Won't that accomplish many of these same goals?**

A: I'm a big fan of yoga and Pilates. At Athletes' Performance, we view yoga and Pilates as specific disciplines, much like golf is a specific sport. Pilates and yoga are great complementary activities to your Core Performance Golf program and can be done on regeneration days, or mixed into your weekly or monthly schedule.

Q: **Will I need to be fitted for new clubs after doing this program?**

A: No. Instead, your body will be able to take advantage of the true potential of those clubs. You will discover that you are a better golfer than you thought now that your body can perform to its peak. This could, however, lead you to want to acquire a new set of clubs to match your new body and refined game.

Q: My kids are just starting to play golf. Should they follow this program?

A: Absolutely. Golf is a lifetime sport and a terrific gift to give to children. In addition, kids can benefit enormously from the Core Fundamentals, which will ensure that their bodies and healthy habits grow along with their games as they get older.

Q: Will I gain or lose weight with this program?

A: Don't get hung up on scale weight. If you step on a scale, it just gives you a number. It doesn't tell you how much muscle and fat you have. I can find two people the same height and weight that look dramatically different because of their body compositions. People might weigh the same in their mid-forties as they did in their twenties, but they might have a lot more fat. Building lean mass is the key to success. To measure lean mass, perform the "pinch-an-inch" test by taking a vertical pinch of your skin by the navel. The thinner the pinch, the better. Become less concerned with weight and more concerned with your ratio of lean mass to fat. With this program, you *should expect* to gain lean mass and lose fat. If you're

someone in reasonably good shape when you start this program, you could gain weight and look far leaner—or as some might say, "skinnier"—losing inches off your waistline. If you're hoping to lose weight through this program, you might not lose as much scale weight as you expect. But since you're reducing fat and increasing muscle, you'll look leaner and end up stronger than with traditional diet plans that promote weight loss, which is usually temporary, without building lean mass.

Q: It's difficult to remember proper form for some exercises. Will it ever become second nature?

A: Definitely. You're developing your body in such a way that you naturally hold these postures and go through these ranges of motion without thinking about them. We're reprogramming your "computer" so that you hold perfect posture and pillar strength, with the shoulder blades back and down, the belly button up and in, and the hips stabilized. If you can do that, you will do the majority of these exercises very well. Once those circuit breakers are activated, they're on. It's like when you walk into a room and turn on the lights. They remain on; you don't have to keep holding the switch. After a while, you'll also bend properly without thinking about form. When squatting or bending, remember to do so from the hips *and* the knees, not at the waist. Remember to sit the hips back and down, using the glutes and quads as opposed to just using the lower back or putting a lot of stress on your knees.

Q: Am I always going to feel so unbalanced and uncoordinated?

A: No. Every athlete I work with, regardless of skill level, feels awkward at first. It might take a few days or even a few weeks, but when you get it, it will change the way your body works. Be patient; it's a new skill. If I were to ask you to do only those things you're good at, you'd never improve. I want to push you beyond your limits. Focus on the process, and the end result will come.

Q: Why won't I get bulky doing this program?

A: Because there's proper balance between the lengthening of the muscle and the stabilization of the muscle. The resistance training will take you through a long, full range of motion, which not only will help build muscle but also improve the length of the muscle, so you have a long, lean, athletic look. And because you're gaining lean mass and losing fat, you'll avoid looking bulky, since a pound of lean mass takes up far less space than a pound of fat.

Q: I travel a lot for business. How can I ever keep up with this?

A: I , too, travel a lot for business. So do the golf athletes that follow this program. Admittedly, there might be times when you won't have access to as much equipment as you'd like, although medicine balls and cable-lifting machines have become common in hotel gyms. Like anything else, it's important to plan ahead. Pack a rope for your AIS stretching. Throw some high-protein meal-replacement bars and packets of post-workout recovery mix in your bag so that you don't have to resort to junk food. If you reach the end of the day and you find you haven't exercised, do something in your hotel room. Go through the Movement Prep routine. Work on some of the core/hip/shoulder stability routines. Take out the rope. It's especially important to work out when you're traveling because of all the stress traveling causes. You're inevitably stiff and cramped from sitting in a tiny airline seat. Your body might be trying to adjust to a new time zone. Do what you can to keep from getting run down.

Q: Is static stretching really bad?

A: Static stretching can be a great tool, when properly timed. The Core Performance philosophy stresses that the warmup, what we call Movement Prep, is active and dynamic. This does not make static stretching bad. Static stretching works by sending a message to the muscle saying, "Shut this tightness off," and it ultimately forces the muscle to release. Static stretching is best used post-workout or later on that day or night to elongate the muscle and connective tissue, while turning off the overachieving nervous system. It is also effective on pure recovery days, even before you warm up. Long static holds help to produce long-term changes in the fascia (the band of elastic tissue that envelops the body, beneath the skin), ultimately improving muscle balance and length.

Q: **What do I do if something starts to hurt?**

A: Immediately identify what hurts, then apply many of the concepts in the book.

Examine your biomechanics, your symmetry from right to left, your pillar strength—and the inner workings of all the systems discussed. Stop doing what hurts, and embark on 3 to 7 days of a regeneration-focused training plan. If the pain has subsided for some time, gradually start training with low volume and take regenerative days off between active days. If the pain persists, seek out a qualified sports physical therapist for hands-on evaluation and treatment. It's much easier to deal with the small stuff than to turn a blind eye and set yourself up for a major injury.

ACKNOWLEDGMENTS

Writing a book, like playing the game of golf, requires focus, determination, and mental toughness. I could not have made it through the back nine without a team of people who have these qualities in abundance.

The staff, athletes, and extended family of Athletes' Performance have inspired the entire Core Performance series and made significant contributions for four books now. A very special thanks goes to Craig Friedman, Amanda Carlson, Dan Burns, and Dave Schifrin for helping to shape the message of this golf program. I could not have written this book without assists from Michael Bentley, Jeff Ritter, Gray Cook, and Scott Peltin. I also owe a huge debt of gratitude to my longtime tag-team partners Pete Williams and David Black, along with Rodale's ever-supportive team of Kathy LeSage, Pete Fornatale, Susan Eugster, Karen Neely, and Colleen Keeffe. As for my wife, Amy, no words can express my enduring gratitude.

INDEX

Boldface page references indicate photographs.

Underscored references indicate boxed text.

ABOUT THE AUTHORS

MARK VERSTEGEN is recognized as one of the world's most innovative sports performance experts. As the founder and chairman of Athletes' Performance—cutting-edge training centers in Tempe, Arizona; Carson, California; Las Vegas, Nevada; and Gulf Breeze, Florida—he directs teams of performance specialists and nutritionists to train some of the biggest names in sports.

By teaching an integrated lifestyle and training program that blends strength, speed, flexibility, joint and "core" stability, and mental toughness, Verstegen helps athletes become not only faster and stronger but also more powerful, flexible, and resistant to injury and long-term back, hip, and other joint problems.

Because of his innovative techniques and up-to-date knowledge of sports performance, Verstegen is a sought-after consultant. He serves as director of performance for the NFL Players Association, is an advisor to adi-das, EAS, and other leading performance-oriented companies, and serves as a consultant to numerous athletic governing bodies.

A dynamic speaker, Verstegen travels the world to address groups such as the American College of Sports Medicine, the National Strength and Conditioning Association, and many corporate audiences.

Verstegen and his training methods have been profiled by hundreds of national media outlets. He's a contributing columnist to *Men's Health* magazine and has written three previous Rodale books. *Core Performance: The Revolutionary Workout Program to Transform Your Body and Your Life* was published in 2004. *Core Performance Essentials* was published in 2006, and *Core Performance Endurance,* in 2007.

Verstegen began his coaching career at his alma mater, Washington State University. He served as assistant director of player development at Georgia Tech and in 1994 created the International Performance Institute on the campus of the IMG Sports Academy in Bradenton, Florida. In 1999, he moved to Phoenix to build the Athletes' Performance Institute, which quickly became the industry leader for training world-class athletes.

Verstegen and his wife, Amy, live in Scottsdale, Arizona.

PETE WILLIAMS has written about fitness, business, and sports for numerous publications, including *USA Today, Men's Health,* and *SportsBusiness Journal.* He is author or coauthor of nine books, including the three previous Core Performance titles (with Mark Verstegen), *Fun Is Good* (with Mike Veeck), and *The Draft: A Year inside the NFL's Search for Talent.* A graduate of the University of Virginia, an avid triathlete, and a popular keynote speaker, Williams lives in Safety Harbor, Florida, with his wife, Suzy, and their two sons and hosts *The Fitness Buff* radio show out of Clearwater. His Web sites are www.petewilliams.net and www.fitnessbuffshow.com.

For more information on Mark Verstegen's Core Performance training programs, including interactive workouts and nutritional information, please visit www.coreperformance.com. The site also offers sport-specific DVD programs for golf, tennis, soccer, baseball, football, and other sports, along with training equipment and information on how to attend seminars and personalized training weeks at his four Athletes' Performance locations.